Master Your Whole Life

Foundation for an Art, Science and Technology of Human Development

Master Your Whole Life

Foundation for an Art, Science and Technology of Human Development

BOB REED

NEW VISION PUBLISHING
Toronto

Copyright © 2000 by Bob Reed

All rights reserved. No part of this book may be reproduced or transmitted in any form or by any means – graphic, electronic or mechanical, including photocopying, recording, taping or any information storage and retrieval system – without written permission from the publisher, except for brief quotations in a review.

Published in 2000 by
New Vision Publishing
The Exchange Tower
130 King Street West, Suite 1800
P.O. Box 427
Toronto, Ontario M5X 1E3
Canada
Tel.: (416) 865-3381
Fax: (416) 947-0167

FIRST EDITION

Canadian Cataloguing in Publication Data

Reed, Bob, 1942-

Master your whole life: foundation for an art, science and technology of human development

Includes index.
ISBN 0-9686390-0-3

1. Self-actualization (Psychology) I. Title.

BF637.S4R44 2000   158.1   C99-901607-5

Cover design: Bheem Maharaj

Printed and bound in Canada

DEDICATED
TO HUMANITY

CONTENTS

1. The Book's Purpose 1

2. Overview — The Three Aspects of Personality 3
   and Seven Dimensions of Existence

3. Using the Rational or Intellectual Aspect to Help in 5
   Self-Unflodment and in Mastering Practical, Day-to-Day
   Existence

4. Meditation — Developing Intuitive Knowledge 23

5. Emotions/Feelings and Qualities: Developing the Positive 39
   Ones and Getting Rid of the Negative Ones

6. How to Strengthen the Will/Power/Action Aspect of Your 63
   Personality

7. Succeeding in the Seven Dimensions of Existence 79

8. Laws or Principles of Success and Human Development 99

9. Integrating/Balancing/Unifying the Three Aspects of 111
   Personality and Seven Dimensions of Existence in
   Day-to-Day Life

Index 121

CHAPTER 1

The Book's Purpose

The purpose of this book is to help bridge the gap between science and technology, and human development. It's because of this ever-widening gap, in which human development has been left far behind, that we're faced with many of our personal crises and social problems. Throughout the world mental disorders have been increasing, conventional religions have been collapsing, family life is in shambles, political and economic systems are in turmoil. We need collective global action to address many of these pressing concerns. However, the action must emerge from a more enlightened perspective to have the desired results. This is more likely to happen if as many people as possible throughout our planet focus on speeding up their development. Then will they be more equipped to help shape their lives and environments in more positive directions.

This book presents knowledge, skills and attitudes that, when mastered, will enable people to integrate personal development with practical achievement. Its main thrust is in guiding the reader to develop a unified or well-rounded personality and achieve greater overall success. It shows how to work with personal development as a systematic and an ongoing process to reverse the historical trend of a piecemeal, occasional approach. It also provides systems, principles, strategies, and techniques which, when consistently and accurately used, will help individuals evolve and continue growing in their day-to-day lives: while working, playing, traveling, interacting with family and friends, etc. In addition, it fuses meditation with the scientific method to assist people in making better decisions and solving problems more effectively.

Those who regularly apply what they're about to learn will: experience greater love, peace and joy; have a more harmonious and satisfying family life; experience a sharpening of their minds and senses; generate greater creativity; motivate others towards higher productivity; create and maintain supportive relationships; be more persuasive; become higher level performers at work, sports or in any other activity; unfold their consciousness to a much higher level; be more mentally and emotionally ready to solve personal and social problems; and live a more exciting life.

Before ending this chapter, may I offer you an assignment which I have given to participants as preparation for one of my seminars. Here it is: "Trace your life as far back as you can remember to the present, identifying your strengths, weaknesses, interests, trends or patterns, major goals, needs, dominant motives, special abilities, and skills." This assignment was designed to help people understand themselves generally and discover their mission in life specifically. While reading the book, pause from time to time and relate the material to the relevant insight about yourself you gained from doing the assignment. Then at a certain point in your reading, your mission or purpose on this earth plane may flash into your mind (if you have not yet discovered your life's purpose). If this happens and you persist in pursuing your true calling, then an exceptional human being will have been born who may eventually make a solid contribution toward the betterment of humanity.

CHAPTER 2

Overview —
The Three Aspects of Personality
and Seven Dimensions of Existence

Analyze human nature and you will see that every person can know, feel, and act. Thus knowledge/wisdom, feeling/emotion, and action/power comprise the three core aspects of personality. Also examine people in their daily lives and you will uncover seven dimensions of existence with which each must come to terms: the physical, mental, emotional/aesthetic, social/family, financial, recreational, and moral/spiritual.

However, humans through countless ages have been developing in a one-sided manner. This has resulted from their neglecting one or more aspects of personality and dimensions of existence. The time has come to correct this situation: to point the way to the creation of the unified person. A unified person may be defined as one who continues to develop the three aspects of personality and achieve goals in the seven dimensions of existence. Whoever succeeds in doing this has a greater chance of mastering all facets of life. Whoever neglects any of these areas will one day experience a crisis and be forced by nature to attend to the unheeded aspect. Why is this so? This is so because these facets of life all have certain basic needs attached to them. For example, people have a need for companionship (social dimension); love (feeling/emotional aspect); a higher meaning to existence (moral/spiritual area), etc. Note the intense suffering caused by many workaholics whose family lives are destroyed through neglect. Mark well also the emotional emptiness of the one-sided intellectual who no longer experiences love or joy.

Having outlined the breadth or framework within which human development should proceed (the three aspects of personality and seven dimensions of existence), let us briefly move into the depth of our position. This will be done by relating the three-aspect model of personality to Truth. First, what is Truth. Truth, for our purposes, is life itself: that pure Force or Energy that is the essence of all life-forms. It is the central organizing principle of nature. A fragment of this Truth, called the Pure or Higher Self, is also the core of our personalities and expressed, in Its untarnished form, as pure knowledge/wisdom, pure feeling/emotion, and pure action/power. Pure, in this context, means oriented toward growth and development.

A further insight into the components of personality will give us a better grasp of what is to follow. It is this: knowledge may be divided into intuitive and rational knowledge; feeling/emotion, in its highest and most refined forms, may be expressed as love and joy; and action/power is at its noblest and most effective when performed with a pure motive and from a profound center of stillness. However, despite its division into three parts, personality must be seen as a whole.

In the twentieth century, life had become too fragmented. Now, at the beginning of the twenty first century, we must work diligently to put it back together again and re-experience our lost unity. This book advocates a unified, integrated, or balanced approach to life — viewing and working with the three areas of personality and sevenfold division of existence in terms of interrelationships and interdependencies. Each element is connected to the other like a chain.

CHAPTER 3

Using the Rational or Intellectual Aspect to Help in Self-Unfoldment and in Mastering Practical, Day-To-Day Existence

A. DEVELOPING A PHILOSOPHY OF LIFE

The twentieth century had been very chaotic and people everywhere seemed to have lost direction. This condition came about because of many factors, some of which had been: unprecedented changes through technological breakthroughs, the breakdown of conventional values and institutions, and incomplete teachings about practical living filtered down to us for thousands of years. Some of these teachings have been inadequate in the sense that, though addressing partial aspects of life, have been handed down to us as complete. This book is written with the purpose of helping to correct the situation by presenting a more comprehensive perspective. Many of the teachings on how to live that have guided humankind's existence were formulated by great teachers centuries or even thousands of years ago. Much of their wisdom is still relevant. But the needs of the twenty first century are, in many ways, different from those of bygone eras. Thus, it becomes necessary to reformulate and creatively fashion things to suit our context.

The time is ripe for us to adopt, in the area of human development, a fresh approach to suit our age. It's wise to stress more self-reliance and an open, experimental approach towards existence. The teacher within should guide us to a greater extent and we ought not to be afraid to challenge any form of authority, no matter how sacred. If something is the truth, it will eventually prevail. We must learn to accept those teachings, no matter how painful, that will help us become better individuals and discard whatever encourages us to violate the dignity of others. To help us, we may question life: ask ourselves what's the best way to live. We will profit greatly by seeing existence from many angles and viewing it in the same way in which our planet is heading through the new technologies – global. To assist us, also, it's necessary to develop a blueprint or philosophy of life. A sensible way to approach this task is by examining our lives and carving out a framework to suit our specific needs. Here are some questions, the answers to which, will constitute our life's philosophy: (1) What is our most important belief and how do we or should we apply that basic belief as an approach or orientation to life? (2) What is our basic assumption of man/woman? (3) What is or should be our basic orientation towards people? (4) What are our most important values or guidelines for action? (5) How do we balance life's polarities?

What follows are the author's answers to the proposed questions. He has tested the helpfulness of these ideas in the battlefield of life for many years. You're free to use all or a part of them if you feel they will help you lead a more effective existence. But whatever you do, think about your life in very concrete and specific terms and work with whatever will enable you to become a more evolved human being while, at the same time, helping advance the welfare of others.

1. Basic Belief Translated into Basic Approach or Orientation to Life

The writer's basic belief is that there is One Truth or Energy Source that underlies or pervades existence. It is our central Reality. This Essence or Truth is manifested through our personalities in three forms: wisdom/knowledge, feeling/emotion, and action/power. Thus, our basic approach or orientation to life should be a balanced and full expression of these three aspects. To express them adequately and creatively, we ought to assume a positive, pro-active stance towards existence. A positive approach or stance means emphasizing the positive in dealing with people and situations, thereby reversing a planetary trend of focusing on the negative. It also signifies turning the negative into positive by learning valuable lessons from seemingly unfavorable circumstances. If you look for lessons with eagle eyes, you'd find them; and these lessons, once applied, will often prove to be your most valuable ones in terms of advancing your inner development and outward success. This perspective also implies an active rather than a passive approach by creatively influencing the environment. It reduces itself to the critical or ultimate point of helping to move our planet in a positive direction rather than being influenced by the planet (certain kinds of people) in a negative way.

2. Basic Assumption of Man/Woman

Man/woman is an open system with vast potential, linked to a limitless Energy Source. This Source, translated in human terms, is like a Cosmic Personality with the three aspects of knowledge/

wisdom, feeling/emotion, and action/power raised to perfection. Our objective is to constantly work towards elevating these three areas of personality in ourselves and guiding others to elevate theirs to this perfected Ideal.

3. Basic Orientation Towards People

Our basic orientation towards people should be development-oriented. Most humans, without realizing it, are depressive-oriented. After communicating with them, if we're not strong enough, we can end up feeling terrible about ourselves and the world. The mass media, so critical in helping shape public opinion, have contributed in this direction by almost exclusively focusing on the sensationally ugly side of life. While the negative should indeed be reported, the media can certainly give a lift to humanity by reporting, to a greater extent, stories and news of those virtues and values that will help improve the quality of our lives. However, at an individual level, we must ensure that our thinking, speech, and action are geared toward helping ourselves and others grow and develop in a more healthy, happy, and productive way. Note that this idea of being development-oriented, if set into motion, can have a revolutionary effect on the practice of management specifically and leadership generally.

4. Guidelines for Action or Basic Values

Carefully worked-out values, especially in times of difficult decision-making, can prove their weight in pure gold. Here are some that will be very valuable in day-to-day living:

i. **T(t)ruth**
ii. **justice**
iii. **excellence**
iv. **joy**
v. **beauty**
vi. **cooperation/unity**
vii. **pleasantness and cheerfulness**

Truth with a capital T is that underlying Principle or Source that sustains or holds together everything and into which everything eventually returns. This book has two primary and inter- related objectives: to guide others to experience this Truth (higher development) and to express It (for practical achievement) in all aspects of their daily lives, so they may become the very best they're capable of becoming.

Truth, with a small t, signifies living our lives in such a way that people can trust us and believe in us. It certainly doesn't mean stabbing others with the truth but being sensitive to the human condition by timing what we must say and saying it in such a way that we'd help the person improve. Note, however, that Absolute Truth (with a capital T) and relative truth (with a small t) are interconnected — one helps in moving us towards the other. However, both meet in the concept of **integrity** which means a wholeness or completion of outlook that impels others to trust our judgment and decisions implicitly.

Justice has always been, and will always be, a critical value in the lives of humankind. It strikes a responsive chord deep within the core of our being. The play of great events in history often centers on justice versus injustice. So important is justice that the legal systems of all countries are based on it. Observe your deep, instinctive reaction against any person who displays injustice against another. Note well this point: if you're a leader or an aspiring leader, fairness or justice should be central to your leadership practice. You will never become great in a sustained manner without it. If you were to trample upon this important law of justice, the wheels of this selfsame justice will one day roll over you.

The value of **excellence** is linked with achievement at a higher level. All works of genius are derived from an inspired Source and usually comes about through a flash of insight. However these, or any other productions of a lesser but still brilliant nature, result from careful, painstaking effort, usually over a long period of time. In other words, we must pay the price in hard work for that creative insight to emerge. Also mastery of any thing or the invention of something comes about after a series of refining and reworking with the irrepressible spirit of excellence forever bubbling beneath the surface of the mind. By focusing on and achieving excellence in whatever we do, we will achieve a greater sense of self-fulfillment and success.

Joy and beauty are twin partners. With intensity of experience comes joy. Joy is born when we've wrapped up in a labor of love, thereby causing time and space to flee and spirit to break through. When we behold the beauty of nature and are absorbed in great works of art, music or painting, we drink from the ocean of joy. Sometimes also we must let go and become like little children in their innocence and playfulness and joy will spontaneously flow. We should also cultivate an eye for beauty which is the revelation of the divine in its physical glory. Joy and beauty may also be experienced and expressed by all of us in realizing our fullest potential in whatever we do and in communicating in such a way that we bring out the noblest and best in ourselves and others.

There is also a pressing need for **cooperation or unity** in our troubled world. Both at a national and an international level we need it to solve the problems of: air and water pollution, drug abuse, crime, terrorism, poverty, and racism. It is likewise necessary at home to build a strong, stable family and at work to foster productivity within a network of supportive relationships. In fact, it is critically important in our times of suspicion and divisiveness at all levels of society. Cooperation becomes much easier when we can understand and perceive that all people are brothers and sisters because of the same Force that binds them into an organic unity.

Finally, the values of **pleasantness** and **cheerfulness** are much needed in a world filled with problems of every variety. We must learn to forget our cares at certain times and reflect on some of the positive things for which we ought to be grateful. We should learn to smile and maintain a pleasant disposition, especially when the going gets tough. For we must remember that, in due course, all things pass away. And we should never forget that other people are like mirrors reflecting our moods. If we're depressed, sooner or later we'd cause others to become likewise depressed. If we radiate cheerfulness, others around us will also loosen up. Life ends up becoming painful if we walk around with an air of seriousness all the time. It's wise to form a balance by experiencing the lighter side of life. Remember the pleasant and cheerful person is a joy to behold, helping to lighten the emotional burdens of those around him and adding to his own happiness.

5. Balancing Polarities

One of the more serious, but often overlooked problems in life, is people going out on a limb: they think in terms of black and white, or mutual exclusiveness. This practice must be examined because it produces negative consequences. One of the ways in which the issue can be resolved is by learning to see many areas of life, not as opposites, but polarities. Then proceed to balance within ourselves and in terms of action these polarities. Examples of polarities or things at both ends of the same pole are:

i. **Rational/Intuitive**
ii. **Unity/Diversity**
iii. **Personal/Impersonal**
iv. **Assertiveness/Passivity**
v. **Cooperation/Competition**

Here is how to perform the balancing act. See the **rational** and **intuitive** faculties as tools to generate the same thing – knowledge. Then when we find ourselves going into one tract by being too rational, let's be still and allow the wisdom flowing from deep silence to surface.

Let's also learn to perceive **unity** in **diversity** and diversity in unity. For example, when we find ourselves having conflicts with others by focusing too much on differences (i.e. race, color, religion), let's remember our similarities: that we're human beings with the same basic needs and there is an underlying unity that runs through everyone's existance.

In addition, when we're becoming too **personal** and find ourselves swayed by biases and prejudices, it's time to switch into being more **impersonal** or objective. On the other hand, too much objectivity in dealing with people causes our relationships to become mechanical. At these times we need to inject some of the finer feelings, such as concern and caring.

We should also be **assertive** or **passive** as the situation requires. For instance, in the heat of an argument or bargaining situation, when we've pressing our point forcefully, observe what's happening to the other person. He/she may feel too pressured and may not want to budge. At this time, pause and remain passive. Carefully observe what he or she is saying and very often a common ground can be found.

Lastly, there's an urgent need to balance the poles of **cooperation** and **competition**. Healthy competition is necessary to spawn excellence in areas like sports and business. However, people throughout the world have become so competitive that it's wise for all of us to consider how we may cooperate to help create a world with heart.

Please note that the basic principle in applying the method of balancing polarities is this: when we find ourselves dwelling too much on one pole and switch to the other, we've automatically bringing ourselves in the middle where all poles meet in a dynamic balance. When we reach that juncture or meeting point, we do so in deep silence from which we move into a subtle unity with the power of the Source.

B. USE OF A SCIENTIFIC APPROACH FOR SELF-UNDERSTANDING AND DEVELOPING STRATEGIES FOR ACTION

The scientific method is the axis upon which the whole of Western Civilization spins. It has been largely responsible for the great scientific and technological breakthroughs we see parading before our very eyes. The use of reason stands at the center of this method. It's this same reason that offers itself to humankind as one of the most important tools in working out our destinies. Our success or failure in life largely hinges on the effective use of it. The following, based on the rational or intellectual aspect of our personalities, will help us in self-unfoldment and in mastering practical, day-to-day existence, if applied as specified:

1. **Action-Research Method or Model**
2. **Developing Strategies/Systems for Action based on the Action-Research/Scientific Method**
3. **The Situational Approach**
4. **Combining the Non-Rational and Rational For Personal Understanding and Faster Development**
5. **Challenging Conventional Thinking**
6. **Feedback from Others**

1. **Action Research Method or Model**

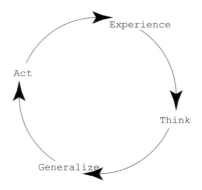

The action-research model is a modification of the scientific method. Here's how it works. Follow the preceding diagram. Whenever you **experience** something you believe is important, **think** carefully about it. Look at it from many angles, drawing out a principle. This is the **theorizing or generalizing** stage. Then, **act** upon that principle or guideline to see how valid it is. While acting you will, of course, have an experience. At this point, again go through the whole process. Start the thinking part by asking yourself whether the principle that you formulated before is still valid, partially valid or not valid at all. If it's still valid, then act upon it again as it stands; if it's partially valid, reformulate the principle and act; if it's invalid, develop a new principle and act. As you act, your experience, upon reflection, will indicate whether your principle is standing up to the rigorous test of practical reality. Go through the process as many times necessary until you're reasonably certain that you have a solid principle you can use. The result of applying the action-research method is a sharpened, alert mind capable of developing guidelines or principles that will help make your existence a more effective and worthwhile one. You may even end up discovering a new scientific law.

2. Developing Strategies/Systems for Action Based on the Action-Research/Scientific Method

The following two strategies were developed by the writer, using the action research method. They came about after thinking through many personal communication encounters with a diverse range of people.

Strategy For Effective Communication

(a) Understanding (Observe content, tone of voice, gestures, facial expression)
(b) Suitability (Say what is appropriate in the situation)
(c) Precision (No wasted words; also, not talking too long)

Strategy For Dealing With Difficult People

(a) Integrity (Try to understand the person's whole situation: feelings, speech, behavior, etc.)
(b) Justice (Reward those aspects of speech or behavior that are desirable; correct any injustices; give feedback and if necessary, exercise firmness on whomever is exhibiting undesirable speech or behavior)
(c) Hope for improvement (Help to rechannel speech or behavior in a more positive direction in an appropriate manner. Bear no malice).

Here is the process through which I went, many years ago, using the "Action-Research Model", to develop the "Strategy For Effective Communication". I once had a serious conflict with an individual which lasted for quite some time (experience). When I went home, I began to think about the interaction (think). I asked myself why did this conflict arise and continue unresolved. Then I realized both of us were not trying to understand each other, but were just intent on pushing through our viewpoints. Thereupon I drew out a principle based on my thinking (generalize). The principle was: to communicate effectively, focus on understanding the other person. To understand, I thought I should ask questions, and observe the individual's communication content, tone of voice, gestures, and facial expression. I followed these suggestions very closely when I had my next communication. The effect was unbelievable (experience). As I forgot completely about myself, I felt a sort of oneness or unity with the person. I sensed at a deep level what he was feeling and thinking. I had a harmonious discussion, even though differences in opinions surfaced once or twice.

I then began to think I had the secret to effective communication. To make sure, I decided to test this principle of deep understanding or empathy. I tried it this time with my wife but ended up in an unresolved conflict with her. I thought carefully about the situation and realized that, though my understanding of her position was correct, I did not respond suitably. Thus, I developed the second principle in the communication strategy: to communicate effectively, respond suitably to the demands of the situation. On the next interaction with my wife, I made sure I not only understood her but replied suitably. This came about through thinking carefully before speaking. This time the result was spectacular. Communication flowed very smoothly, though we had to resolve several difficulties in the process.

Now I thought that with the principles of "understanding" and "suitability", my communication strategy was complete. I was wrong. On another interaction, though I used these two principles, the communication attempt ended up in confusion. On reflection I realized that, on that occasion, I was too long-winded. I felt the person had lost tract of what I was saying. As a result, I formulated the third communication principle: to communicate effectively, get to the point as concisely and clearly as possible. On my next communication I used this principle. My contribution was brief and to the point. It worked as intended. Communication was very effective. However, I did not neglect to use the other two principles.

Thus, this is the way I invented the principles that make up the "Strategy For Effective Communication". May I assure you that the "Action-Research Model" is a very powerful tool for accelerated development. If you were to use it in the manner indicated above, your quality of insight and degree of effectiveness in day-to-day life will improve measurably.

3. The Situational Approach

To be effective, you must respond to the demands of specific situations. To do so, you should understand the situation by analyzing the elements involved and responding appropriately. Generally, here are some of the main factors or elements in most situations: the people involved (including yourself) — their background, needs, intentions, styles, values; the issue or task to be worked on, including goal(s) and method(s); the setting or environment (formal, informal, rigid, open, etc.).

I know a businessman who has developed the effective habit of looking at issues from many angles and asking such penetrating questions that he quickly gets to the heart of the matter. His approach has helped him over the years to beat the competition and close many seemingly impossible deals. He has mastered the situational approach in business. He makes sure he understands the need or needs of the person(s) involved. Then when he's discussing the issue, he relates what he's offering to the need(s) of the other(s). If it's an informal or more structured environment, he operates accordingly. At several points in the discussion, he tailors his speech, silences, and behavior to the specific demands of the situation. The result is that he's much more successful than most of the others in his line of business. Yet this same person is always having conflicts with his wife. While he uses the situational approach at work, he neglects to do so in his family life. His wife is much more emotional than rational. Thus, she feels interrogated and uncomfortable with his constant questioning. Having discussed the situation with him, he now tempers his questions with greater caring, love, and appreciation. His wife has become much more receptive to him and he's now getting similar results with his family as he does on the job. The situational approach is a master key for helping to achieve success in perhaps all areas of life.

4. Combining the Non-Rational and Rational for Deeper Understanding and Faster Development

Take a sheet of paper and write everything that comes to your mind. Don't censor anything; let it flow. This method will dredge out material from your subconscious or unconscious. Then think through carefully what you have written to understand your deepest thoughts. After doing this exercise several times, you will get more in-depth knowledge of yourself. Unconscious material must also be taken into account to get a fuller understanding of yourself. Remember, don't feel guilty if terrible things surface. Everybody has some of those stored away. After analyzing the material seek, where necessary, to purify your thoughts and emotions to evolve to a higher level of development. Make sure you tear up the paper after each session if you can't keep it in a safe place, for you will most likely not want anyone to see your completely uncensored thoughts.

5. Challenging Conventional Thinking

Truth needs no crutches. If it's the T(t)ruth, it will eventually win out. Don't, therefore, be afraid to question any form of authority. A questioning approach is one of the best ways to understand most things. If Columbus did not question, where would we be today? If Einstein did not question some of the seemingly iron-clad findings of Newton, we perhaps would not have seen the dawning of the atomic age. We should not only question authority, but life itself. If we do, we're more likely to find out the best way to live it. If we don't, life will interrogate us with greater trials and tribulations. For, what we do not learn through reflection, nature forces upon us in sorrow.

6. Feedback from Others

Get honest, straight feedback about yourself from someone whom you trust and who cares about your development (i.e.) a good friend, husband, or wife. The other person can also be helped if the feedback is mutual. Then use the feedback to improve yourself. Sometimes the information might be painful, but remember that very often the bitterest medicine brings about the cure. You will be stunned at the remarkable progress you can make through feedback on a regular basis. Your personality will become more and more refined as those annoying mannerisms and tendencies drop off when someone points them out to you in a true spirit of love and helpfulness. Often these bad habits become so habitual that you do not notice you're displaying them.

I once observed a certain individual constantly having conflicts with others. On asking myself why this was happening, I realized that he always looked at the negative side of things. Whenever someone came up with an idea, his first reaction was to shoot it down. After getting to know him well and was reasonably certain that he trusted me and valued my opinion, I pointed out his habit. I became surprised to learn that he was doing this for many years (according to the reports of others) without realizing it. Gradually I used different methods to encourage him to see both the positive and negative aspects of issues. My feedback had a dramatic effect on his personality and the quality of his interactions with others.

A few years ago I did a screening interview with a person for a job. He's a chartered accountant and also has an MBA. At several points during the interview he would put his right hand over his mouth. I debated with myself whether I should tell him about it, reasoning that this habit could prevent him from getting the job. I was about to send him to be interviewed for a position with a very large and prestigious company. I finally decided to let him know. He was not annoyed but was very grateful for the feedback. Apparently he had developed this habit for many years and no one had ever mentioned it to him. He made sure that he didn't put his hand over his mouth during the interview with his prospective employer. He ended up getting the job. The interviewer was impressed not only with his academic credentials and work experience but also with his natural, alert manner during the interview.

CHAPTER 4

Meditation — Developing Intuitive Knowledge

A. AN EXPLANATION OF MEDITATION AND CONCENTRATION WITH EXERCISES IN CONCENTRATION

1. Meditation

The main purpose of meditation is to realize Truth or the Pure Self. Other names for Truth or the Pure Self are Pure Consciousness, Pure Mind, the Real Self, the Higher or Actual Self. This Higher Self is pure energy and is part of the Central Energy Source or Absolute Truth that underlies all existence. This Central Energy Source or Cosmic Energy Field may also be called the Force, Source, Truth, Absolute, Supreme, God, or Mind. From It everything came and into It everything goes. Its nature, within a human context, is Energy, Intelligence, and Purified Feeling/Emotion. Thus, it can be expressed in the forms of action, knowledge, and love or joy.

The apparent self or ordinary mind is an energy complex comprising thoughts held together by the reflected light of the Real Self. To get to this Actual Self, dissolve thoughts and allow this borrowed light to re-unite with the Pure, Original Light. The concept of the borrowed light can be more clearly grasped if one understands the nature of the light coming from the planets revolving around our sun. These planets do not have light of their own but still give off light. Their brightness is simply light reflected from the sun.

The advantages of realizing this Pure Self are: peace, joy, love, increased intelligence, creativity, and energy. In addition, the quality of insight begins to develop more powerfully. This insight often occurs to geniuses, such as great scientists, writers, composers, painters, etc. It is precisely at times of these intuitive flashes that exceptional or revolutionary ideas are born. Yet you don't have to be a genius to experience insight. Everyone does to a certain extent. However, by learning to still thoughts at will, everyone may frequently experience valid solutions to problems through intuitive flashes which, of course, must be tested in the crucible of day-to-day existence. The most effective way to help these insights emerge is to go through a process of careful thinking on valid information. They come when you're silent or not attending to the problem and often at an unexpected time. The training in meditation (the stilling of thoughts) may be fused with the scientific method (objective reasoning on valid data) to help you live a more successful life.

2. Concentration

Concentration is critical in all forms of meditation. It is governed by two laws: the law of curiosity and the law of interest. Curiosity, in the sense in which it is used here, means a passing or superficial interest. It is different from the genuine curiosity of the true knowledge seeker. The former type of curiosity stems from the nature of the ordinary mind or self which is restless. It naturally tends to flit from one thing to another. The mind, operating at this level, is like a ship tossed about on the ocean by a mighty storm. It's as though someone, holding a handful of mustard seeds, suddenly flings them into the air. These scattered thoughts rob you not only of energy but achievement. At the end of the day when you're tired, you're more mentally exhausted than physically tired. Just as many tributaries flowing out of a river sap the energy (water) out of the main body of water, likewise stray thoughts drain you of your energy supply.

The law of interest is the other side of this law of curiosity. Whatever absorbs your interest will cause your mind to remain fixed at that point. When this happens, the mind merges with the object of attention and the Higher Self or Pure Mind takes over. Thus, the ability to concentrate is necessary before you can master meditation. In fact, "sustained concentration" is a good definition of meditation. Note also that if you wish to generate interest in anything, think of all the advantages of pursuing it.

3. Concentration Exercises

Here are some exercises that will greatly improve your power of concentration.

(a) Use of the five senses: actual and imagination practice.
  i. **Sight:** Look carefully at a still object, then close your eyes and see it in your imagination. For example, if you're looking at a pen, first examine it part by part. Estimate its length and shape, determine the color, feel the texture with your fingers, and look closely to see if there are any special marks or scratches. You will find yourself becoming more and more interested and absorbed in the

object. Then, be silent for a few seconds. Next, take in a good visual impression of the whole pen and continue looking at it naturally for about five minutes. You may gradually extend the time with practice. Afterwards, close your eyes and see the pen in your imagination. Visualize it as clearly as you can for about one minute. Then the exercise is completed. The visualization time may gradually be extended. You may do the same exercise with an object in motion. If you're using the same pen, move it from side to side across your field of vision, while looking at it. Again, close your eyes and see the pen moving in your imagination. You may set your own time limit. Note that when your concentration becomes stronger, the exercise can be done with two or more objects.

ii. **Sound:** Listen to any sound in your environment. It may be a sound like the whirring of a fan, the playful noise of a child, or chirping of a bird. Then move away where you can no longer hear it. Now listen to the same sound in your imagination. If there is no naturally-occurring sound, create one. For example, tap a pen or spoon on the surface of a table. Afterwards stop and again do the imagination-practice.

iii. **Taste:** Taste something and when the taste fades from your tongue, again taste it in your imagination. It may be some honey, a piece of fruit, a few grains of nuts, or anything with which you feel comfortable.

iv. **Smell:** Smell a scent, then smell it again in your imagination. It may be a whiff of perfume, the fragrant scent of a rose, or anything of your choice.

v. **Touch:** Rub your index finger over the texture of any object several times, carefully observing the resulting sensation. Then stop and go through the whole process in your imagination. Make it, as in all the other exercises, as intense and vivid as possible.

vi. **Feel:** This exercise is to be done with an emotion, preferably a positive one such as love, joy, happiness or compassion. As you experience an uplifting emotion, while perceiving something or interacting with someone, focus and feel it as deeply as possible. Prolong the feeling for a while. Then when you're away from the thing or person, re-experience the emotion in your imagination, capturing and savoring the rich, energizing feeling.

(b) The preceding exercises showed you how to concentrate at the physical and emotional levels. This one deals with the mental dimension. Do it this way: **develop a flow of interrelated thoughts on a theme** (i.e.) love, joy, beauty, integrity, excellence, or any practical concern that's important to you. Your concentration is broken only when a thought, unrelated to your theme, enters your mind. When this happens, get rid of the stray thought and move back to what is relevant. Mastery of this form of concentration has tremendous implications for intellectual success and power.

(c) If you were to practice the above exercises diligently and regularly, you'd be startled at the vast improvement in your power of concentration. However, one of the main aims of this book is to help you integrate development into your day-to-day life. Thus, the final exercise in concentration is no exercise at all. It's about living a concentrated life. Concentrate on existence itself – on whatever you sense, perceive, feel or do. Be alert to the mood and behavior of others; enjoy the magical beauty of nature; concentrate while eating, dressing, walking, exercising, writing, etc. – be aware or conscious of every movement. However, let the concentration be relaxed and natural, and your awareness and enjoyment of life will be greatly improved. Why will you get these results? You will make contact with and operate from the Force or Higher Self within you. Concentration is the magic tool or device that brings this about.

B. RELAXATION AND MEDITATION EXERCISES

1. Relaxation Exercises

i. Visualize your body like a rag doll. Hang your head to the right, loosening the neck muscles. Next, lean your head to the left, again relaxing the neck muscles. Then droop your shoulders and let go your arms, allowing these parts to fall into a relaxed state. Afterwards, let go the middle part of your body; then do the same with your legs. Finally, feel your whole body loose and limp like a rag doll.

ii. Relax your body, part by part, from head to toe while counting from 1 to 10. Start by saying one, all the nerves, fibers, and muscles of my head are falling into a calm, placid, serene state of relaxation. Two, all the nerves, fibers, and muscles of my face are falling into a calm, placid, serene state of relaxation. Continue in this manner until all your body parts are covered. Follow up in this order: Three, repeat the same statement for the neck; four, the shoulders and arms; five, the chest; six, the stomach; seven, the buttocks; eight, the legs; nine, the feet; and ten, say all the nerves, fibers, and muscles of my whole body, from head to toe, are falling into a calm, placid, serene state of relaxation. If, by this time, your body is not completely relaxed, scan it in your mind until you locate the part or parts that are still tense. Then let go the area or areas into a loose, relaxed state.

iii. Stiffen and relax your body from toe to head. Again, do part by part. This exercise is based on a certain law of nature: the **tension-relaxation law**. It simply means that if you were to tense a part of your body and then let it go, that part will automatically fall into a relaxed state. Do both the tensing and relaxing in a gradual manner. First, tense both feet by pointing your toes downward; then let go. Tense them again, this time by pointing the toes backwards. Let go. Follow through by stiffening and relaxing your legs, buttocks, stomach, chest, shoulders, arms, neck, face and head. Then, when you're finished, look over your entire body, searching for any tense spot. If you were to find one, do the exercise on this part until it's relaxed.

iv. Picture your body like a bag of grain (any kind of grain). The mouth of the bag opens and the grains gradually pour our.

While this is happening, feel your body becoming limper and limper with relaxation.

Comments: These relaxation exercises can be of great practical value to you in your daily life. For example, you may do one or all of them if you're tense and/or nervous before an interview, a business meeting, a rehearsal, a speech, etc. You will notice that your body and mind are closely connected: once your body is completely relaxed, your mind will likewise fall into a relaxed state.

2. Meditation Exercises

The following exercises may be done singly or as a sequence in the order given.

    i. **Heart:** First, close your eyes. Then, meditate in the heart area. See a lovely, white rose there. The petals gradually open and blue smoke comes out. Hold the image of the rose, and as the smoke slowly rises, feel your consciousness merging with the smoke and drifting upwards. After a while, let go the image completely and be silent. Then gradually open your eyes. In fact, for all the meditation exercises, open your eyes in this way, else you may experience discomfort if your eyes are suddenly exposed to the light. You may be asking why a white rose and blue smoke. White symbolizes spiritual purity; and blue, intellectual brilliance. Thus, the intellect is here merged with the spiritual element through the use of colors.

ii. **The Mantra OM:** Meditate on the mantra OM while counting. Silently say OM 1, OM 2, OM 3 until 10. Then start again in the same way counting up to 10. Continue for three sets. Then stop. Begin once more, only this time do not count. Just keep saying OM very softly. Then stop repeating it and remain silent. This mantra is considered sacred in the East where It has been meditated upon for thousands of years. It's a word and sound symbol that represents the Absolute or the Source from which everything came. You may, however, wish to make up your own mantra. For example, Christians may prefer to use love and Moslems, Allah.

iii. **Breath:** Meditate on the breath, counting from 1 to 10 and stop. Continue for three rounds. Count one for an inflow and outflow of breath. Then focus on the breath without counting until you can sense it no more or until it has considerably slowed down. Finally, maintain a prolonged silence. Note that as your breath becomes stiller and stiller, your thoughts get fewer and fewer until the mind also goes into a state of deep stillness.

iv. **Third Eye:** Meditate on the third eye area. This is the region between the eyebrows. It is the spiritual eye from which you sense things without the aid of the normal five senses. It is the source of inspiration and extra-sensory perception.

v. **Above the Head:** Meditate just above the top of your head. First, make contact with your consciousness inside your head at about the temple area. Then gradually move the consciousness upward until it's just above the head. Hold it there. Now move it slowly outwards until you feel it touching the four walls of the room in which you're sitting. Sense the expansiveness for a while. Next, gradually gather the consciousness above the head again. Meditate on it for some time, then gradually draw it within your head. Remain silent for a while, not meditating on anything at all.

Comments: While meditating you do not have to sit cross legged as the Easterners, if doing so makes you feel uncomfortable. Just sit comfortably on a chair. The best times to meditate are early in the morning, just before supper, or close to your bed time. However, you may meditate anytime it's convenient. About half an hour is generally sufficient time. Some people get best results with one hour of meditation. Experiment to see what is the ideal time for you. There are no hard and fast rules. However, if you can spare only ten minutes, by all means, practice for ten minutes. Close your eyes while meditating. Remember also the intensity of concentration is more important than the length of time spent.

C. DEEPER MEDITATION EXERCISES

1. **Inner Breath:** Put you right thumb into your right ear and your left thumb into your left ear. Place your first four fingers on your forehead with the little fingers resting gently upon your closed eyelids. Then focus on your breathing. Latch your mind onto your breath and flow with it. Your breath will

seem unusually loud at first but will gradually slow down until it's barely perceptible. When you can hardly hear your breathing, just remain silent before ending the meditation.

2. **Inner Sound:** Follow exactly the same instructions for the previous meditation (the one on inner breath), only this time forget about the breath. Concentrate instead on the inner sound. Keep attending naturally to this sound. In the beginning the sound will appear loud but as you concentrate, it will become gentler and gentler until you can barely hear it. When you reach this point, become silent again for a while before opening your eyes.

3. **Who Am I:** This meditation is excellent for those who are intellectually inclined. However, it may be done by anyone. Close your eyes and silently ask yourself the question: "Who or what am I?" Then follow up with the other question: "Am I my body?" Then reason in this way: The body lasts for a lifetime and is gone. But the "I" is eternal. Thus, I'm not my body. Again ask: "Who or what am I?" "Am I my emotions?" My emotions are fleeting, they quickly come and go. But the "I" is eternal. Thus, I am not my emotions? Now for the third time question yourself: "Who or what am I?" "Am I my thoughts?" My thoughts are likewise short-lived, coming and going with extreme rapidity. But the "I" is eternal. Thus I am not my thoughts. Then conclude by saying: I am not my body but the master or controller of my body; I am not my emotions but the master or controller of my emotions; I am not my thoughts but the master or controller of my thoughts.

I am eternal, beyond time and space, and the element that holds together and sustains the body, emotions, and thoughts. "Who or what am I?" With this last question, merge all the forces within you into a deep state of silence and listen for an answer. By doing this meditation regularly, a time will come when you may have a clear and direct answer to your question and your true identity will then be revealed. Remember that when nothing seems to happen on the surface, you're still making progress at a deeper level. If nothing else, this form of meditation is usually followed by profound peace.

4. **Consciousness Looking Down:** See your consciousness looking down from above your head at your body. Dis-identify yourself from the body, as though your body belongs to someone else. It does - it belongs to Pure Consciousness or the Actual Self. Identify with this Consciousness or Force, for you are It.

5. **Space:** Meditate on space. How do you do it? Visualize your consciousness gradually traveling for millions of miles though space. Then feel your consciousness becoming one with space itself. Sense an enormous expansiveness. Next, let go everything and plunge yourself into a very deep silence. Become one with silence itself. If this exercise is done with deep concentration, the experience is unbelievable, truly out of this world.

6. **Silence:** The last part of the previous exercise fulfils the requirement of meditating on silence. In reality, all of the

preceding meditations should end with a letting go into a state of silence. Actually, silence is the technique of the masters. It's difficult to accomplish, but once experienced by stilling all thoughts, a state of blissful harmony results. It's necessary to practice silence to overcome the tyranny of uncontrolled thoughts. If you find it difficult to maintain silence, do the following exercise. Use the second hand of your watch to practice. Start with a time convenient to you, whether it's 10, 20, 30 seconds or more. During this period, you must be free from thoughts. If any thought enters your mind, stop the exercise and start over. Gradually extend the time to 1, 2, 3 ... 5 and up to 10 minutes over a period of weeks or even months. Once you can be in a silent or thought-free state for 10 minutes, you will have accomplished an unusual feat. Not many people can do this. Besides, whenever you're in a state of genuine silence, you are making connection with the Source or Spirit. Your Higher Self will then be operating. In addition, you will now be on the road to sustained higher development and greater practical achievement. For you will be able to direct powerfully your controlled mind towards the achievement of any goal.

During training and consulting sessions, I have had the opportunity to coach others on how to use silence as a tool to improve their lives. An example readily comes to mind. It involved the president of a corporation with whom I was doing personal consulting. Of all that I taught him he loved working with silence the best. At the time he felt intense mental pressure because of the nature of his work. I suggested to him that after every fifty-five minutes of work, whenever possible, to practice silence for five minutes. I advised him to use the second hand of his watch to time himself. At first, he found it extremely difficult to remain silent, as thoughts kept swirling through his mind. However, as the days went by, he found himself doing it more and more easily. Of course, sometimes he would be in the middle of a meeting and thus unable to do the exercise. Yet the results were amazing. After three months practice, he felt greater mental alertness, experienced more valid insights into issues, and generated higher quality work.

D. CONCLUDING REMARKS ON MEDITATION

Meditation is a natural process. Every individual spontaneously experiences it during odd moments. Whenever we're absorbed in the beauty of nature, wrapped up in a piece of enchanting music, or immersed in a delightful task, we have entered a meditative state. At these times we experience Pure Awareness or the Higher Self. Unlike these occasional moments of absorption, the intent of the previous exercises is to get us into a state of meditation consciously and regularly whenever we choose.

The peace and harmony that result after a successful meditation are worth the effort. Besides, we need to refresh ourselves spiritually on a day-to-day basis to meet the challenges of our fast-changing world and defeat stress. Remember that we're already connected to this Absolute Truth or Cosmic Energy Field. However, because of our heavy cares and tribulations, we have lost awareness of the connection. Meditation helps us bring back that lost awareness. Once we rediscover our divine nature, all things become possible. We will then have free access to the Source of all wisdom, love, and power. Our insights will be more accurate. We will experience all people as brothers and sisters. And our actions will move in a continuous flow, enabling us to do difficult tasks with less effort. We will have become a channel for that Supreme Power that pervades and upholds everything.

CHAPTER 5

Emotions/Feelings and Qualities: Developing the Positive Ones and Getting Rid of the Negative Ones

A. BACKGROUND INFORMATION

1. The Origin of Emotions

Humans are highly emotional beings. However, negative emotions, which are widespread, tend to impair one's functioning. But positive emotions, such as gladness and affection, meet with the approval of all. Yet psychologists, who're experts in human behavior, point out that your chances of successful living are better if you're not at the mercy of even these emotions.

John B. Watson, founder of the behaviorist school of psychology, did several experiments on small children. From the results of these tests, he discovered that infants show three basic emotional reactions or responses. These reactions he called "fear", "rage", and "love". He claimed that these were the basic emotions from which the more complex emotions of adults came about.

However, as a result of further tests by other psychologists, it was discovered that fear and rage or anger are really different forms of a single emotion. This emotion was called "excitement". For example, Mendel Sherman, another psychologist, found out that fear and rage were difficult to distinguish when observing the outward behavior of children. He made his discovery from an experiment he conducted with medical doctors, psychologists, and student nurses observing an infant. For instance, only 4 out of 31 of them judged that the infant's reaction was fear when they did not know the child was falling. However, 27 out of 31 called it fear when they saw the baby being dropped.

Research in anatomy also confirmed the idea that only one **basic emotion**, "excitement" exists as opposed to the condition of calm. We may say then, that at birth, the infant expresses (1) excitement (2) calm pleasure. The latter response puts the child in a state of equilibrium or harmony. The former causes him to be imbalanced.

As the child begins to grow up, his general excitement branches off into distress and delight. Then distress develops a cluster or family of emotions and so does delight. Distress splits itself into emotions like jealousy, disgust, fear, and anger. Delight offshoots into elation at first and later, joy.

We may also understand emotions from an historical and a physiological standpoint. We find the first "fight-flight" of "human nature" in our primitive ancestors. The two emotions of anger (for fight) and fear (for flight) were useful in ancient times. As primitive man faced an opponent (survival of the fittest), he showed anger. When he met a greater danger, fear was the reaction. These two emotions resulted from insecurity or a threat to the individual's harmony or balance. They were used to help satisfy the most basic need for survival or self-preservation.

Here's what happened. When our ancestor felt a man or animal too powerful to overcome, he began to experience fear. The emotion of fear was relayed to the pituitary gland (this gland is affixed to the lower part of the brain). The gland then released hormones which caused the adrenal glands or "glands of combat" (one each located on both kidneys) to get excited. These hormones also caused the liver to discharge sugar into the blood stream. What happened at this point? The heart began to beat with greater strength and speed. The lungs dilated, causing the person to breathe more rapidly. This resulted in greater use of oxygen, as high as 25% over the normal amount. The supply of oxygen quickened and the release of carbon dioxide was also fast. His blood pressure increased, speeding blood to his leg muscles. Thus, he was able to run away very fast and avoid danger.

On the other hand, when our ancestor stood up to fight for his life, the emotion of anger caused identical physiological reactions. Only this time the energy coming from the blood's sugar went to his arms instead of his legs. Thus he was able to defend himself better.

However, in our so-called "civilized culture", fear and anger do not serve valuable purposes. They interfere with our thinking which is the best tool for dealing with problems. Both these emotions exist in the modern forms of worry and resentment. If you worry, you're afraid of someone or some situation. Whenever you resent someone, you're angry with him. It appears that the central source of most negative emotions is anxiety, a painful uneasiness about the future. Thus, to have faith is crucial to mental health. Make your choice: either live a life of faith or fear. Perhaps the wisest course of action is to do your best and then accept, with a calm mind, whatever life offers. The only thing you can really do is keep on trying and hope that in the end all will be well.

Please keep in mind that this writer is not saying to give up all emotions. He believes that the more refined and pure emotions like love, compassion, and joy are necessary to help us express our fullest humanity. It should however be noted that love is a special case: it's an emotion which also includes a state of calmness and unity. Sometimes, too, constructive discontent with our present condition is essential in pointing the way to upward movement or achievement. In addition, some anger in the form of passionate concern against injustice can serve as a spur to take suitable action against this form of crime.

2. Negative Emotions and Qualities: Main Blocks to Development

The root of human suffering and greatest hindrance to human development or self-unfoldment is viewing yourself and/or functioning **Out of Context**. This happens when you see yourself and/or function as an isolated unit, rather than being connected to a **Larger Field**. The central quality that shows you're out of context is egotism (being too wrapped up with yourself, while leaving out others). Another word for egotism is selfishness which is different from one's rational self-interest that also takes others into account. It is to be noted that from egotism there develop the following twenty (20) negative qualities and emotions which are the main stumbling blocks to self-unfoldment. These must be overcome to scale the higher levels of human development.

The 20 Main Negative Emotions and Qualities

1. egotism
2. anger
3. hatred
4. revenge
5. malice
6. mercilessness
7. injustice
8. impatience
9. intolerance
10. fear
11. worry
12. imprudence
13. vanity
14. dishonesty
15. hypocrisy
16. envy
17. greed
18. lust
19. cowardice
20. undependability

How do these negative qualities and emotions flow out of egotism? Here are some, among many different ways. The **egotistic** person is easily hurt by criticisms or adverse comments, and perceived snobbery. When he feels wounded, he develops **anger** towards the other person. Anger causes him to lose his reason, which is perhaps the most important personal tool for solving problems. As the anger continues, it hardens into **hatred**. Then **revenge** is the natural consequence. When carried to extremes, revenge can destroy both persons. An individual who's bent on revenge will say and do **malicious** things to his "enemy". He will show **no mercy** and the principle of **fairness or justice is thrown to the wind. Impatience** and **intolerance** will come between him and the other. At this point he feels justified in his speech and behavior. He does not, of course, examine his attitude and reaction. Then, he may start developing **fear** and continue to **worry**, as his opponent retaliates. At this point, the first person may retreat in fear or sometimes lash out in blind fury by indulging in **imprudent** or foolish remarks and/or actions.

Egotism is also directly connected to **vanity**. The vain individual may overdress, wear excessive jewelry, boast about his material possessions or achievement to boost his ego. He may indulge in **dishonesty** (stealing and/or lying) or **hypocrisy** (pretending to be what he's not) to keep up the show. In lying and not being sincere, the person violates the important principle of truth which makes it difficult for him to advance psychologically and spiritually. In addition, **envy** builds up when the egotistic person realizes that he can no longer show off. Why? Someone may face him who has more material possessions or a higher level of achievement than he does. Of course this other person, who may have displayed **greed** by accumulating excessive possessions, may also use his wealth to boost his ego.

How is **lust** related to egotism? With lust the individual is seeking his own pleasure, with the other person simply being a tool to satisfy his need. He/she violates a force that binds everyone together – love. If lust alone exists, after the sex act both individuals often tend to lose interest in each other and sometimes experience self-loathing. But love mixed with sex results in a powerful bonding of two human beings.

Lastly, we come to **cowardice** and **undependability**. The coward is too concerned about his personal safety and runs away from even mildly threatening situations. The brave person faces danger squarely and sometimes succeeds in a big way because of his courage to take risks. And the undependable individual is egotistic in the sense of being unconcerned about the time and effort of others. He often keeps other people waiting long beyond the appointed time or does not show up. He's not a person to honor his word. Soon others may avoid him or stop doing business with him and when he fails, he's surprised. He then feels the world is giving him a raw deal.

The Effects of the Preceding Negative Emotions and Qualities

a. Emotional

They throw the individual out of balance and cause a lack of peace. When this happens for long periods of time, happiness is impossible.

b. Mental

They cause reasoning to be impaired. Thus, reason becomes a blunted tool for solving problems: objective analysis of facts becomes very difficult. In addition, negative emotions and qualities form the base for mental disorders.

c. Social

These negative qualities and emotions result in disharmony in human relations, causing verbal conflicts, tension, and even violence. At a more serious stage, destructive forces are released and evil spins out of control. World Wars 1 and 2 are classic examples.

d. Moral/Spiritual

They also cause us to be Out of Context or isolated rather than help us experience a sense of unity or wholeness.

e. Physical

Psychosomatic medicine has shown that persistent negative emotions can result in illnesses such as ulcers, migraine headaches, frigidity, impotence, rashes, muscular cramps, high blood pressure, asthma, arthritis, kidney troubles, diabetes, etc.

3. Some Positive Emotions and Qualities: Helping Factors in Development.

The greatest remedy for human suffering and the greatest aid toward human development or self-unfoldment is to view yourself and/or function **In Context**. When this takes place, you feel you're connected to a **Larger Field**. The central quality that indicates you are functioning in context is **integrity** which may be defined as wholeness, connectedness, or completion of outlook. From integrity we get some of the main positive emotions and qualities or virtues like the following.

Some Important Positive Emotions and Qualities or Virtues for Development

1. prudence
2. patience
3. persistence
4. assertiveness
5. love
6. compassion
7. decision making
8. enthusiasm

Prudent people think before speaking or acting. Thus, their speech and action are in tune with the demands of the situation. They talk neither too much nor too little. Commanding the attention of others through wisdom and sound judgment, they help light the path of others in our chaotic world.

Without **patience** and **persistence** nothing great can ever be achieved. Success comes about through a patient, persistent, day-to-day effort. For example Thomas Edison, perhaps the greatest inventor of all times, was the incarnate of patience and persistence. He made about 10,000 experimental tries before inventing the incandescent light bulb. Anyone who's so persistent deserves to succeed. Nature makes sure he does. Also, in terms of dealing with people, patience is a useful virtue. Everyone is different in terms of their background, level of intelligence, and ability. Thus the patient person is rewarded by understanding and good relations with people. Whereas the intolerant individual causes serious conflicts and antagonisms among himself and those with whom he interacts.

Assertiveness is different from aggression. It means not allowing others to take advantage of us. It signifies claiming what is due to us and standing up for what we believe. It certainly doesn't mean pushing our weight around, unmindful of the rights and feelings of others. If someone is getting out of hand in an unreasonable way, it may be necessary to exercise a certain degree of firmness.

Love will forever be a central value so long as we remain human beings. It's the highest expression of the emotional side of our nature. We're all spiritual brothers and sisters by being connected to the same Force or Source. Thus, we ought to love that Divine Spark in all, which Spark is the essence or core of all humans. By so doing we're loving everyone without condition, though we need not love the speech, attitude, or behavior of those who're working on the negative side of life. Remember that taking steps to defend ourselves when we're in danger does not mean we're giving up the principle of love. But we must defend ourselves without malice; we should correct situations without anger; and allow nothing to disturb our mental balance.

When we're bogged down by the cares and trials of life, when we find ourselves becoming too negative, we should stop and take hold of ourselves. Then practice the following exercise: send out vibrations of love towards those who're close to us in our immediate environment. In fact, this is an excellent exercise to do at certain times during the day even though we're in a good frame of mind. We may also emit vibrations of love to our spouses, children, friends, etc., even though they may be far away. Love transcends time and space and serves as a powerful unifying force. This love technique, when practiced sincerely (yes, even love must be practiced), will have a positive impact on our lives in terms of how good we feel, how good those affected feel, and the more positive reactions we get from them. Consider the implications for all sorts of human relationships: marital, work, social, etc.

Love is the balmiest of all virtues. It's like a refreshing breeze and a fountain of renewal. It's a force that binds us into a sublime unity. Maybe at the end of our lives, the ones we remember most may be those who loved us the most. No doubt this love survives death and moves through the folds of eternity.

Closely related to love is **compassion**. This virtue is necessary on our planet that's so filled with suffering. Sometimes a kind word, a little helping hand, an honest smile will make a world of difference. Remember that no one knows what destiny has in store for us. In our turbulent times, wealthy men have lost their entire fortunes overnight.

Decision making is critical in our modern age. To achieve our goals or succeed in anything, we must make decisions. The average person wavers too much. He/she lives a life of continual indecision and ends up as a failure. When we can't even get off the ground, how will we ever hope to succeed? Even when some people make decisions, others discourage them and they give up.

Thus the surest way to become a winner, to rise above the average, is to make firm decisions based on objective information and realistic analysis. To do so, we must gather as much information about the issue or topic, from as many different sources as possible. If we still find it too difficult to decide, get a blank sheet of paper and draw a straight live down the middle. Then on one side put the word "advantages" and on the other, "disadvantages". Next, after having filled in all the advantages and disadvantages, make a decision based on the side with the most reasons. Afterwards, follow through with action. If we do this, we'd become much more successful. Note also that before making a final decision, we should turn the problem or issue over in our minds and look at it from all possible angles. In addition, while generating ideas, don't use reason alone but rely also on insight by listening deep within ourselves in silence.

Enthusiasm comes from deep sincerity in what we're saying or doing. It's born of a strong conviction and is necessary for great success. It becomes very contagious. Our enthusiasm spins out strong positive vibrations and spills these on others. When this happens, we'd find people believing in us, supporting us, and working with us. Many will be drawn towards us like a magnet. But this enthusiasm must ring through our voices, shine through our faces, and spark with our actions.

B. AN ORGANIZED OR SYSTEMATIC APPROACH FOR CONQUERING NEGATIVE EMOTIONS AND QUALITIES AND BUILDING UP POSITIVE ONES

The following is an organized or systematic approach for conquering negative emotions and qualities and developing positive ones.

1. Dynamic Positive Method

The dynamic positive method uses positive suggestions and action to bring about personality changes. The following four techniques flow from this method.

i. Mirror Technique

This exercise involves looking at your face in a mirror. Get a good visual impression of it. See a friendly face. If it's not friendly, smile. Feel relaxed. Then accept yourself as you are, with your strengths and weaknesses. There's no one like you in the world. You're special. Thus, really learn to like yourself. At certain times during the day you'd see your friendly, pleasant face and will get an emotional lift. Remember, however, to forgive your faults but continue making efforts to overcome them.

ii. Positive Imagination Technique

Go over some of your happy and/or successful experiences. See them vividly in your imagination, just as if they're happening right now. Capture the winning feeling and joyous experience associated with them. Don't forget to relive each event step-by-step, clearly visualizing the details. It may be the thrill of hitting a home run; the rapture of experiencing an uplifting piece of music or a beautiful scene of nature; the self-fulfillment you feel in doing an excellent job; or the joy of talking with a kindred person.

Successful and/or pleasant experiences are the foundation of a strong, healthy personality. Whatever experiences you have leave a neural electrical tract in your brain. (The brain is a chemical-electrical system). Strengthen the positive tracts to be happy and success-oriented. Repetition is the key. You become what you think all day. Weaken the negative tracts by starving them. Be sure not to repeat the negative ones in you imagination. Reverse the normal process – people keep on reliving their negative experiences. That's why most of them are unhappy and unsuccessful.

iii. Imagination Action Technique

Imagination is the eye of the Higher Self, the spark of that Supreme Power within you. Whatever you constantly visualize will come to pass. Thus, picture yourself in new situations acting with the qualities you wish to develop or achieving your desired goals. If you want to be brave, see yourself in your imagination acting bravely. If you wish to hit a home run, visualize yourself striking the ball over the fence. See the ball zooming through the air. Feel the impact of the bat against your body as you hit the ball. And hear the roar of the crowd, as you feel that thrill of elation rising within you.

iv. Action Technique

Act with the qualities you wish to cultivate. For example, if you want to be more attractive, smile radiantly; if you wish to become more generous, share more readily what you have. Also, whatever you fear to do, go ahead and do it. By cultivating the appropriate habits, your fears will disappear. Fear is simply an internal reaction to an external situation. Usually your emotions control you. But action can control emotions. Now you may control and determine your emotions by acting with the qualities you wish to express.

In addition, indulge in physical action when anger is boiling up too strongly within you. For instance, go for a brisk walk or quick run. Play tennis and give that ball some powerful slams. Punch a punching bag. In fact, do anything that will work out the steam. If you don't, the tension and frustration that result from anger may cause you to insult someone or knock him/her down. In addition, if you repress the rage, you may develop psychological problems and/or even physical disorders like high blood pressure and skin rashes. It's best to admit to yourself that you're experiencing a negative emotion when it's happening and then find a way to deal with it.

2. Dynamic Reversal Method

In the dynamic reversal method, the negative is reversed to its positive equivalent. There are also four techniques that make up this method. They are:

i. Instant Reversal Technique

As soon as a negative thought or emotion enters your mind, replace it by its opposite equivalent. If this is difficult to do, use repetition. Say the positive thought or emotion over and over until it turns into a pleasant emotion. For example, if you feel anger for someone, think of, and feel self control. The secret is to attach the strong feeling to a positive emotion or quality. This requires a powerful and instant swing of attitude. If the anger still persists, repeat the word "self-control" over and over until you actually feel control over yourself. Do the same with all negative emotions like hate, envy, greed, etc. Let the positive current flow through you to experience well-being and constructive dynamism. Starve the negative current that interferes with your emotional health and overall effectiveness.

ii. Imagination Reversal Technique

Relive unhappy and failure experiences in your imagination. However, reverse the situation. For example, where you felt fear, see yourself acting bravely. Where sadness was present, let it be replaced by joy. Where you hated, experience love. Where unnecessary mistrust prevailed, trust must reign.

With this technique, you're changing your past experiences from negative to positive. This is an unusually rare opportunity, though the change is taking place only in your mind which is central to your reality. It goes without saying, however, that the past events themselves will not change but only your reaction to them. And as far as anyone is concerned, their reaction is what's important in determining sadness or happiness.

iii. Rational Technique

Reason with yourself to swing from negative to positive feelings. For, your thoughts affect your emotions. When you feel fear due to a threatening event which you believe might take place, make a logical appraisal of the situation. Then deal with it in the best way possible. Say to yourself that you'd change what you can and leave alone what you can't. Prepare, if necessary, for the worst. Often you'd discover, after the situation has long passed away, that your fear was based on confused thinking directed at straw persons. You'd even laugh at yourself for having worried over nothing.

iv. Affirmation Technique

To reverse any negative emotion, relax and repeat a positive equivalent of the negative statement you have silently been making to yourself. Do this over and over until you feel good. Whether you realize it or not, whenever you experience an emotion, you quietly say something to yourself before. For instance, if you feel hate for someone, you might have made statements like these prior to your feeling: "Here comes the bore again. Isn't he a big show off? Does he ever irritate me! I wish he'd leave me alone." If you were to find yourself saying these things and getting yourself in a negative mental and emotional state, say instead: "I respect him because of the same Truth or Force that resides in both of us. In me there's room for only good will towards all people. If he's showing off, he may be making up for being humiliated earlier on in his life." Remember that repeated suggestions get into the subconscious and bring about personality changes according to the nature of the suggestions. Of course, if you can't get along with the individual, politely excuse yourself. Also, it does not mean you should allow people to walk over you. Sometimes firmness is necessary in dealing with people whose behavior is harmful.

3. Equilibrium Method

Whenever someone says or does something to upset you, relax, be silent and put your mind in a state of balance or equilibrium.

With this technique, you neutralize the negative emotions, but don't entertain positive ones. You just remain balanced in silence. The quickest way to reach a state of harmony or balance is to operate from that center of stillness within.

4. The Seven Day Program Using The Success Blueprint

To cultivate a virtue or eliminate a fault, use the following outline or blueprint for seven days in a concentrated manner. Here is the Success Blueprint.

a. **Goal**
b. **Course of Action**
c. **Obstacles and How to Overcome Them**
d. **Projected Time**
e. **Progress**

Here is an example of how I used this success blueprint or goal setting guideline during one week in the year 1975.

a. **Goal**

To live in continuous inner silence and do everything with full concentration. Note that "continuous inner silence" does not mean a lack of thoughts all the time. When it's necessary to think, you must do so with thoughts. However, this continuous inner silence is maintained when you can sustain an ongoing flow of awareness with the rise, duration, and ebb of thoughts. In other words, you begin to have conscious control over your thoughts which you can direct at will.

b. **Course of Action**

   i. Practice in live settings every day.

   ii. Write down goal on a piece of paper and read it out aloud three times a day: morning, noon and night. The goal in written form is: "I will live in continuous silence and do everything in full concentration." Also repeat the goal periodically during the day.

   iii. Do imagination practice.

c. **Obstacles and How To Overcome Them**

   i. Haste

   ii. Lack of control of thoughts and emotions

   iii. To overcome i. and ii. repeat the catch phrases "continuous silence" and "full concentration" everytime the mind wanders.

d. **Projected Time**

   7 days: from July 23, 1975 at 8:00 a.m. to July 30, 1975 at 8:00 a.m.

e. **Progress**

   i. Do an ongoing commentary on progress.

Day 1:

   i. Did three hours of non-stop intellectual work using the continuous silence and full concentration techniques or catch phrases as specified in (c) above. I used these techniques periodically for about fifteen minutes and afterwards my mind stopped wavering.

ii. Had to hurry a revision of a lesson on goal setting, I was about to teach, in ten minutes. However, through concentrated use of both catch phrases, especially the full concentration one, I experienced concentrated speed instead of haste.

iii. Meditated for about half an hour and had better results than the day before. Overall, my mind was focused but there were a few lapses here and there.

iv. Experienced difficulties in controlling my mind while on bed. Dreams were not too good. I tried to use the techniques but found my mind still spun out of control.

v. Used the imagination action technique by picturing myself reading a new book, fully concentrated. After doing this imagination practice for only about ten minutes, I felt powerfully concentrated. Then I actually read the book. This concentrated attention lasted for quite a while. My mind didn't waver at all. What tremendous power is locked up in the use of the imagination!

Day 2:

i. Looked outside at a leaf and then at a flower. I concentrated fully. I was no longer feeling the restless pull of the mind. I suspected that the imagination practice done last night was helping my concentration in this live situation.

ii. Did morning meditation for about an hour using the two techniques. Felt some improvement but my mind was still wandering.
iii. Read a book for about one and a half hours and was reasonably concentrated. At periodic times when my mind began to stray, I stopped and said, "full concentration" and was carried through for long periods with the momentum. Then at certain moments, I repeated, "continuous silence" with the same positive effect.
iv. Went to the park with two of my sons. While there enjoying the beauty of the crystal clear water from a stream, a thought came to me. The insight was that by maintaining continuous silence (no thought distractions), I was being led to a center of stillness somewhere within me. I experienced a connection to some kind of Energy Field, feeling a continuous flow just like the water of the stream that I had shortly left behind. Then as my mind began to wander, something told me to latch it to the breath. When I did so, I noticed that my mind became very concentrated again. I continued focusing on the inflow and outflow of my breath. The breath faded and once more I felt myself light and peaceful and in a total state of awareness.
v. Read for about an hour. Verbalized again the phrases "full concentration" and "continuous silence" at periodic times. Concentration was becoming more and more powerful. Later on during the reading, I seemed to focus naturally on the essence of both phrases without verbalizing. I felt somewhat freer and again very concentrated.

vi. On bed last night and this morning I had much greater control of my mind. I silently verbalized "concentration" instead of "full concentration" and "silence" instead of continuous silence.

vii. Noticed that with a controlled mind, the images of people with whom I had conflicts no longer entered my consciousness. As they tried to enter, the two techniques tended to push them out. I experienced a greater state of mental freedom.

viii. Coined the phrase "concentrate in silence" to replace both techniques. I also used the word "concentrate" as a mantra. The word "silence" can also be used as a mantra. I was becoming more and more focused.

ix. Mind was lapsing into absorption with trivial thoughts. Caught myself in the act and said that my whole life should be a continuous thread of concentration.

x. Concentrated on the lush, green vegetation outside and the melodious chirping of birds. At first, I felt like moving away in haste to attend to a task on which I was working. However, I got rid of the temptation by saying to myself that I didn't know when I'd stop focusing on these aspects of nature. I gradually became totally absorbed in the beauty of my surroundings. I lost all awareness of time and space. I was suffused with joy. At an unexpected time I discontinued and went away. Thus, I controlled and directed the mind into an area of my choice instead of being controlled by a restless flow of thoughts.

Day 3:

i. Read for one and a half hours using the expression "concentrate in silence" periodically. After this time period I felt fresh and new as though I had done no mental work at all.

ii. While meditating, I stopped using the phrase "concentrate in silence", as this verbalization began to become burdensome. At odd times when my mind attempted to wander, I simply paused and brought it back on stream.

iii. Noticed that my mind was becoming naturally concentrated on everything I did. I felt a sense of heightened awareness and joy. My mind was then like an obedient servant instead of a tyrannical master.

Day 4:

i. Woke up this morning feeling great. Before, my mind used to be somewhat out of control at this time. Now it was remarkably controlled.

ii. Felt concentrated while reading, working on a project, shopping in the supermarket. Concentration was becoming a habit.

Day 5:

i. Worked with lightening speed at a piece of writing but my mind remained focused – no techniques were used.

ii. Went to a movie. While being seated I experienced an unusual sensation. I felt as though I was growing like a giant and towering above everyone in the audience.

Day 6:

    i.   Concentration continued to stabilize.

    ii. A lapse occurred. I spoke to one of my students for about an hour and a quarter. He had a lot of problems. My concentration was broken at certain times. I felt a bit tired afterwards. However, the tiredness was short-lived.

Day 7:

    i.   Wrote from 7 a.m. till noon. Was completely concentrated.

    ii. Throughout the day I took part in all kinds of activities: sports, writing, teaching, etc. and felt a continuous flow of concentration. Powerful concentration with a silent connection to some kind of Energy Field within me seemed to be stabilizing at a subconscious level.

CHAPTER 6

How To Strengthen the Will/Power/Action Aspect of Your Personality

1. WORK CONTINUALLY TOWARDS WORTHWHILE GOALS

The human brain is like a computer: whatever you put into it consciously or unconsciously will be processed and a response will be given based on the inputted material. Your brain organizes this data that comes into it continually from all sides into goals or objectives. This is because the brain is naturally goal-directed. This fact has staggering implications for success or failure.

Why are most people failures? A large part of the answer is that they leave their minds idle. Thus very often stray, negative thought-emotions come rushing in to fill the gap. Without realizing it, these damaging thoughts are processed and goals of failure or unhappiness are realized. For example, if you're going for a job interview, you may find yourself silently making statements like these to yourself without being aware of doing so: "It's difficult to get a job these days. There's always a flood of highly-qualified applicants. Maybe, I won't get the job like the last time. What's the use? Everything seems so hopeless, etc." These thoughts will combine with many more negative ones in your memory bank and will cause your subconscious to believe that you wish to fail. Thus, you achieve the goal or objective of failure.

Your mind is also like a garden in which weeds and useless shrubs will grow if you do not cultivate it. If you clean your garden, plant trees that bear flowers and/or fruits, use fertilizer, water it and allow the sunshine to come through, you will reap beautiful goals of flowers and fruits. Likewise if you cultivate the garden of your mind, you'd reap goals of success and self-fulfillment.

It's therefore in your best interest to cooperate with nature and work continually toward goals or objectives of your choice: goals of success in finance, love, joy, peace, good relations with people, etc. In other words, deliberately and consciously make your life a goal-directed one.

How do you set off that process within you for success, and not for failure? Focus on what you want and disregard what you don't want. For instance, before going for a job interview, you may do the following. Learn as much as possible about the company, read about effective interviewing techniques, think about all your strengths in relation to the job, visualize yourself asking and replying to specific questions in a way that impresses the interviewer(s), and keep on repeating statements of success. By doing these things, you greatly improve your chances of success. You also regain your lost freedom by controlling your thoughts and focusing them into desirable outcomes instead of being controlled by stray thoughts into undesirable ones. This principle of concentrating your mind on whatever you choose is the foundation of success in all areas of life. It may be used in sports, education, family life, work, etc.

2. BE PROACTIVE

Being proactive means taking a dynamic approach to life by making things happen and dealing with difficult people and situations in a firm manner. Central to it is the principle of justice. If you're embedded in this principle, you won't let others take advantage of you, nor would you take advantage of others. You'd fight for your rights intelligently and help others fight for theirs.

The following are some specific things you may do to bring out the will/power/action aspect of your personality. Whenever you're listening to anyone, figure out the central meaning of what the person is saying and ask well-directed questions in terms of that meaning. If you're in an interview or among people socially, be proactive and also ask questions. Don't sit passively and wait.

Seek to generate interest within yourself and others. You may do this by offering stimulating and helpful ideas where necessary. Be alive: create excitement around you. Seek out new and creative ways of doing things. When you talk, emphasize key words by raising you voice. Sometimes when you want to catch the interest of someone, lower your voice so the person will lean forward to hear. Vary the pace of your speech. Use well-directed pauses. Take ownership for your ideas and opinions. Develop a firm handshake, walk erect but in a natural way, breathe deeply, move with an air of self-confidence but not arrogance. And don't forget to maintain a positive mental attitude at all times. These ideas will help you develop an engaging personality and bring out the power from within you.

Proactivity is also shown by taking a leadership role in something you feel passionate about. There is a great shortage of effective leaders in all areas of life. Through your initiative in bringing others together to work in a worthwhile field of activity, you can help make this world a better place in which to live.

3. BE ACTION ORIENTED

Knowledge by itself is not power but applied knowledge is: that is, knowledge organized and set into motion. However, whenever you're taking part in an activity, here's the most effective way to act. Act directly — with no thoughts in-between. That is, blank out all thoughts and move to your target from a center of stillness within. Inside you is an Energy Field that releases its power most forcefully when you're acting from a state of deep silence or stillness.

Without action it's impossible to succeed in anything. Too many people miss greatness because their ideas remain only at the planning stage. Revolve in your mind over and over what you wish to achieve. Set down your goal or objective. Work out an intelligent plan and organize your human, financial, and material resources. See yourself in your mind succeeding, and repeat positive self-affirmations of success. Then act with all the energy at your disposal. Don't wait for everything to be just right. This may never happen. Of course, don't rush blindly into anything but don't wait too long either. Many people delay so much that sometimes others seize their ideas and become run-away successes. You must claim and benefit from what is rightfully yours, but to do so you should take action.

4. USE FEEDBACK TO CONTROL AND IMPROVE SPEECH AND BEHAVIOR

Feedback in interpersonal relations means telling the person how their speech or behavior is affecting you or others. This is a powerful and effective, yet neglected tool for influencing people. For instance, many individuals are daily hurt by the insensitivity of others. Some of them bear the hurt in silence; others lash out in blind rage. Both responses often do not get the problem solved. If, however, the anger-response brings about a solution, much bitterness is generated. How, then, do you deal with these instances of insensitivity? You may do so by giving appropriate feedback. Say objectively what the individual said or did. Be sure to describe the speech or behavior. Don't express value judgments about the person's personality, such as, "You're a terrible person, a fool, a bigot, etc." Then, express how he or she is affecting you. Say, for instance: "When you say or do that to me, I feel dumped upon, unfairly treated and hurt." Very often the person will backtrack and stop tormenting you. If he or she does not, then specify the consequences: say what you're going to do or have done if the individual does not stop. Then take the necessary action to resolve the situation. Remember, however, that legal action should always be a last resort.

5. BE OTHER-CENTERED

Most people find themselves bogged down by petty fears, anxieties, hates, frustrations, desires, etc. One of the great secrets of freedom and success is releasing yourself from self-centeredness and sometimes adopting an other-centered approach. How is this done? It is accomplished by focusing your attention outwards and seeing things from the angle of vision of others.

Being other-centered helps greatly in achieving success through people. Here is an example. In business, the most sales are made when you're customer-centered. With this approach you treat customers like royalties. You show keen interest in their needs and wants. You treat them with respect and exercise patience in dealing with them. The result is often satisfied and repeat customers who sometimes bring along friends the next time around.

Notice also that some of the most successful companies are market-oriented rather than production-oriented. That is, they find out what people need, and then cater to those needs. Thus, their products sell swiftly and they make large profits. This is unlike the production-oriented approach in which some manufacturers churn out an enormous amount of products, assuming people will buy them all. They don't go out into the market place to find out what's happening with the consumers. The result is that they sometimes end up with large inventories, much of which they may not be able to sell. In this connection, observe the spectacular rise of the Japanese who find themselves so close to the customer that a number of years ago some corporations in Japan began the practice of inviting consumers into their boardrooms to discuss their needs and get feedback on product performance.

In psychotherapy when the approach is client-centered, attention is focused on the client and not the therapist. The latter does not lecture to the former but listens most of the time. The client, being thus encouraged, unburdens his mind and often arrives at deep insights into his problems on his own.

In adult education, the best teacher is a facilitator who helps participants share experiences and do their own learning from these experiences. Merely lecturing tends to fill people's minds with information, most of which they soon forget.

Regarding human relations, being people-centered instead of self-centered pays rich dividends. You get into the frame of reference of others, understand them and learn to respond appropriately. You thus develop an attractive personality. How can you learn the knack of standing in a person's shoes, while feeling and thinking along with him/her? You'd succeed if you ask yourself two simple questions and probe deeply to find the answers. The questions are: "How is the individual feeling right now?" and "How is he/she seeing the issue or problem from his/her specific frame of reference?"

Finally, to be other-centered as a leader means to care deeply about the needs and feelings of people while they work towards the achievement of goals or objectives. The leader makes sure there's a network of supportive relationships within which the task is done.

When you're other-centered, the following qualities naturally surface: empathy, love, patience, and objectivity. You also find yourself saying and doing what's suitable in terms of the needs or requirements of the situation. You extend your consciousness and become one with people. Apart from the experience of oneness, you sense a refreshing taste of freedom and joy. This is because you snap the chain of selfishness or wipe away egotism or the influence of the lower self which is the main stumbling block to personal development and social success.

6. CONCENTRATE POWERFULLY

A concentrated mind is the essence of personal power. The quality of "intensity" is one of the main elements in the personalities of outstanding people. The great mystics, artists, scientists, etc. tend to be so intensely absorbed in their work that hours upon hours go by without their realizing what time it is. They often lose track of not only time but transcend space and sense a unity or connection to a Higher Field. At these times they feel energized and empowered. In addition, the superhuman strength and speed of great athletes result, to a large extent, from their strong focus. The power in their concentration is like the intense beam of a welding torch that burns its way through the toughest metal. Here is a simple method to help you perfect concentration. Though it was mentioned before, it needs to be re-emphasized. It is: make it a habit to concentrate on everything you do. This will assist you, not only in mastering practical existence, but will lead you to control your thoughts and thus move you more easily into a field of pure consciousness or higher development.

7. PRACTICE REGULARLY

Mastery of anything is best attained through daily practice of it. The **law of effort** is one of nature's great laws. If you wish to be among the best in anything, practice day in and day out in an organized and systematic way. Do it little by little, step by step, moving on to greater and greater complexity. Develop patience: every time you fall, get up and move on. Persist to the end and one day you may wake up and find yourself an outstanding success in your chosen field.

The power of daily practice struck this writer very forcefully several years ago when he was looking at a television program. Being interviewed was the current world champion in billiards. The announcer asked him how he became so proficient in this particular game. He explained that when he was very young - then in primary school - he had to wait for his father in a recreation hall every day for about half-an-hour after school. As the days went by, he became more and more bored until one day the idea came to him to walk over to the billiards table located in a corner of the hall and poke around the balls. This he did and continued doing. At first he was unable to pot the balls into the holes even after many attempts. However, as time went by he found himself hitting the balls into the pockets with little difficulty. However, what really gripped this author's attention was when the champion began to demonstrate his skill. He used the one ball to strike the cluster of balls and one rolled into a pocket. Then he proceeded to pot the balls one by one without missing any. He sent in the balls using the stick in front of him, at the back of him, at the side of him. He even closed his eyes sometimes while making the shots. But always he put in the ball. At the end of the demonstration everyone was looking electrified at an empty billiards table with this grand master smiling and taking for granted a truly remarkable feat. Regular practice is indeed one of the royal roads to success.

8. APPLY THE LAWS THAT UNLOCK THE SUBCONSCIOUS

The power of the subconscious is awe-inspiring. Unlocking this power is one of the great secrets of achieving any goal: acquiring a virtue, passing a test, perfecting any skill, creating something new, becoming wealthy, developing positive relationships, etc. The following are the four laws that may be used to release the potential of the subconscious: relaxation, verbal self-suggestion, imagination, and faith.

a. Relaxation

The mind and body are connected. As you relax the body, the mind also falls into a placid state. It's when you're in this calm state that suggestions can bypass the critical, conscious mind and move to the level of the subconscious. The most opportune time to suggest anything to yourself is just before going to sleep or just after waking up. At these times you're in your most relaxed and receptive state. Here you're in the hypnogogic state – between sleep and wake, a time when suggestions will move directly into the subconscious. And as the subconscious accepts and believes what you feed it, it will throw out a plan for you to realize your goal.

b. Auto Suggestion or Verbal Self-Suggestion

Usually it's difficult to convince your subconscious mind of anything. This is because of the many negative experiences you've had in your life. Failures, frustrations, fears, worries, anxieties, and self-doubts have daily been plaguing humankind. Thus, if you wish something positive to sink into your subconscious, it's necessary to repeat it many times. Thus, whatever you want your subconscious to bring into fruition, write on a piece of paper and repeat morning, noon and night and even in between those times. In some cases you don't need the statement in writing, just keep repeating it to yourself. As these sentiments move deeper and deeper into your subconscious through countless repetitions, the time will come when your subconscious will believe implicitly in what you say. Then your personality or situation will become transformed in the direction of your affirmations.

c. Use of the Imagination

The imagination is perhaps your most powerful faculty. It operates through pictures or images that continually register and flow on the screen of your mind. If your imagination is not controlled, your thoughts or images will be mostly negative. The impact on you will be the development of failure patterns; a weak, negative self-image; and a frustrated personality. This is the lot of most people.

Never forget that you become what you think all day – the thinking being simply the thoughts or pictures that move through your mind. This statement has awesome implications for your destiny on the earth plane. Therefore, you may influence and control the direction of your life by allowing the imagination to focus on goals of your choice. For example, if you wish to be wealthy, determine what sum of money constitutes wealth for you, whether it's a hundred thousand, a million or more. See the sum vividly in your imagination and picture yourself feeling the texture of the money and owning it. If health is your goal, visualize yourself exactly as you will like to be. If being more loving is your aim, see yourself in your mind's eye responding to others with deep understanding, caring, and helping them satisfy some of their pressing needs. These visualizations may also be done three times a day and even more. As your subconscious is eventually made to erase all barriers to success through powerful visualizations, it will come to accept your goals and show you a way to achieve them.

d. Faith

Faith and action are directly related. Whatever you totally believe or have faith in, will come to pass. However, it's difficult for people to believe suddenly that they can achieve all those worthwhile goals. So it's necessary to work at developing faith. To help you, remember that you're a spark of that Supreme Power that controls everything.

Then, if you really want something, develop a strong urge or desire for it. You may do so by feeding yourself verbal self-suggestions about the thing and visualizing yourself already having it. With repeated affirmations in the forms of auto suggestion and visualization, desire will build up and mix itself with faith so powerfully that life will show you a way to get what you want. However, you must take action on the suggestions coming from the subconscious, else nothing will happen.

Examples of How the Laws or Principles of the Subconscious Were Used

The power of faith struck me very forcefully when I was about 18 years old. I was having a shower when a sharp pain wracked my stomach. It kept going on and on. I wreathed in agony, thinking I might die any minute. Suddenly an inner voice told me that I should tell the pain to go away but should do so with complete belief that my request would be carried out. The next thing I knew was that I was telling the pain to go away with such faith and intensity that it just vanished. I then felt an unusual peace flowing through me.

I also recall that in 1976, I wanted to make $10,000.00 from a seminar in personal development and practical achievement that I had developed the year before. I had conducted it twice but only a few people had attended. I was relatively new to the seminar business. Recruiting these individuals had taken a lot of interviews, time, and effort. Now I was meeting rejection after rejection, so I decided to use the principles of verbal self-suggestion and visualization. I repeated to myself morning, noon, and night, and in between for two weeks that I'd make $10,000.00 through this course.

I also visualized over and over the seminar room having a certain number of participants with myself giving an enthusiastic presentation to a highly receptive audience. Nothing happened for the first week but coming to the end of the second week, the subconscious threw out the reply. It told me to talk to the personnel manager of a retail chain whom I knew very well. After speaking with him he introduced me to the president of the company who asked me what was my line of business. His question provided a perfect opportunity for me to explain my course. And did I ever make use of that opportunity! I can still recall the flavor of the meeting very vividly. This president became so excited with what I had to offer that he promised to send all his managers and directors to my program. He kept his word and I soon found myself training 34 persons who thoroughly enjoyed the seminar. The amount of money I made totaled $10,200.00 (34 participants x $300.00 each).

Another interesting situation arose while conducting a training program for executives. I met an individual who told me he had failed an accountancy exam six times. He claimed that while in the examination room he was paralyzed with fear and couldn't think straight. However, as soon as he came out, he could easily answer all the questions. I advised him to start using the visualization method the same day in mental preparation for his next exam which was three months away. He had to see himself in his imagination writing the exam, being in a pleasant and highly energized mood, and answering every question correctly. He did this practice diligently for the three months, repeating it morning, noon, and night, and at odd times during the day. About a year later I accidentally met him. We began talking and he enthusiastically told me what a miracle had happened in that examination room. He had followed my instructions to the letter. Then, as he began to answer the questions, he felt himself empowered and just breezed through everything. He ended up getting an A. Note carefully what happened. The brain does not know the difference between something vividly imagined and actually experienced. So it assumed that the person in question had already got everything correct with his repeated visualizations, thereby causing him to bring about the same results in the actual situation. Of course, visualization alone won't work. It must be backed up with consistent work.

On another occasion, the chairman of the board of directors of an up and coming corporation attended one of my seminars. When he entered the training room he looked very worried but, on leaving, he appeared highly energized. The lesson taught that night was how to tap the power of the subconscious. The cause of this person's dejection was that his organization wanted to buy the majority shares of another company but was competing with some business heavy-weights. He thought that his firm did not stand a chance. However, he strongly felt that the session had given him renewed faith in himself and had shown him a way to achieve his goal. About three months later this same person came up to me with an extended hand and beaming face. He broke the good news – his company had in fact bought out majority shares of the other firm. I was curious to know what method he had used. He told me that he had employed the auto suggestion and visualization methods in a social context. He got together with the members of his board and all of them silently repeated to themselves that they would achieve their goal. In addition, they visualized themselves already controlling the targeted company. They continued their practice every day for about a month. He explained that coming to the end, their faith was built up so strongly that they sensed very deeply that they would win and they did. Their collective subconscious threw out a strategic idea that did not occur to their competitors. This idea, when implemented, made the big difference.

CHAPTER 7

Succeeding in the Seven Dimensions of Existence

INTRODUCTION

Humans are goal-seeking beings. Goals are heavily influenced by needs or motives. For example, when people are hungry, they strive to achieve the goal of hunger satisfaction. When they're starved for recognition, they often say or do things for others to praise him. Thus, they're able to satisfy the goal of feeling important. When they feel a sense of inner emptiness, they look for something that will give their lives meaning. Therefore, if you wish to live in conformity with your self-nature, make your life a goal-directed one.

Get yourself into the habit of setting goals and working diligently towards achieving them. By doing this, you'd be greatly motivated to succeed. The motivation will become yet stronger when you challenge yourself to achieve greater and greater success. You may lead yourself into this pattern by setting small goals, such as praising instead of criticizing others for the next day. Or set the goal of spending one hour in loving communication with your family today. You'd discover, to your great surprise and joy, that by constantly setting goals and accomplishing them, your life will become much more focused and meaningful. You'd be a greater all-round success.

No matter who you are, your life should be well-balanced and integrated. No area of existence should be ignored. Therefore, you must set goals and achieve them in the seven areas or dimensions of life. These areas are: physical, emotional/aesthetic, mental, social/family, financial, recreational, and moral/spiritual.

Use the following guidelines in setting goals. (1) Write down your goal(s) (2) Your course(s) of action (3) Your obstacles and how you'd overcome them (4) The time you'd take to accomplish your goal(s) (5) Evaluate your progress (6) Reflect on your goals accomplished.

(1) Your goal(s): Before writing down your goals, try to understand yourself. Then, figure out what is likely to help you become successful and give you the greatest happiness.

(2) Course of action: Think about your goals very carefully. Visualize them and repeat them with a positive mental attitude. Then write down, based upon insights from the subconscious and logical thinking, exactly how you're going to accomplish these goals.

(3) Your obstacles and how you'd overcome them: You must also recognize and wipe out effectively all obstacles that arise between you and your goal.

(4) Projected time: Set a definite time by which you hope to achieve your goal. Deadline dates usually spur people to work faster and with greater motivation. Have a combination of short-term, mid-term, and long-term goals.

(5) Progress status: At periodic times, write down your progress. This interim success will serve as a powerful motivator. Also, evaluate your progress to date. Are you performing effectively and on time? If not, what are you doing wrong? What must you now do to speed up your progress and/or do better?

(6) Goals accomplished: State what goals you have achieved so far. Are they giving you the satisfaction you expected? Now set and pursue other goals based on a new perception of existence, else you'd begin to stagnate and lose meaning in life. Remember that a sure way to live a self-fulfilled life is to be an ongoing participant in it, while enjoying everything you do. That is, make every step toward your goal a goal in itself. For example, many students set their sights on the degree or diploma alone and labor on. However, on the day of graduation, when they receive their degrees or diplomas, they're disappointed. Those, however, who enjoyed working towards their credentials had been happy all along. Their award came as a bonus.

A. PHYSICAL DIMENSION

Your body is relatively important. It has to last you a whole lifetime. So, don't neglect it. Besides, if you feel physically weak or ill, your functioning in all areas of life will be impaired. Sound health is essential to your happiness and future progress.

You may develop and maintain excellent physical health in four specific ways: by eating well-balanced meals, by exercising regularly, resting adequately, and keeping your mind positive.

Well-balanced meals

Let's first deal with food. Food provides the biological energy to preserve life, maintain cell and tissue growth, and perform activities. To be strong, fit, and healthy is a great advantage in doing the many kinds of work during a lifetime. The food we eat is the primary means of keeping the body in the right condition.

The three basic components of food are: carbohydrate, protein, and fat. These are called macronutrients as contrasted to the micronutrients of vitamins and minerals which are derived from certain types of carbohydrates. The key thing to remember in eating, as in all areas of life, is balance. Some nutritional schools of thought advocate eating excessive amounts of carbohydrates and very little protein. Others take the opposite position. They recommend consuming a high-protein diet to the neglect of carbohydrates. Both approaches, in the end, will result in health problems. You should eat more carbohydrate than protein, but not considerably more, while focusing on a diet low in saturated fat. You generally don't have to worry about the fat content, as your regular meals will normally have much of what you need.

Carbohydrates are important in providing energy for the body, especially the brain which uses two thirds of that energy. The best sources of this macronutrient are fresh fruits and vegetables which also deliver the bulk of our vitamins and minerals. In addition, they contain lots of fiber which is useful for colon health and proper elimination of waste matter through the bulking of stool. Fiber also slows the entry rate of glucose in the bloodstream. (Note that all carbohydrates not already in the form of glucose must be broken down into this shape to be able to move through the blood.) This fiber-control is critical because if the carbohydrate enters the bloodstream too quickly, it goes into the adipose cells and is stored as fat and remains there as fat. The carbohydrates that don't have as much fiber, vitamins, and minerals are grains, starches, and pasta. Thus, eat these foods in moderation. Eating more fresh fruits and vegetables will generate greater health.

Protein is just as important as carbohydrate. Its building blocks are amino acids, which form the foundation of all life. Only water is more plentiful in the body than this macronutrient. About half of your dry body weight is made up of protein from which every cell in your body is built. Protein is needed to build and repair your various systems: immune, muscular, cardiovascular. It is also useful in synthesizing hormones, repairing tissues, transporting oxygen to your cells, digesting food, even thinking. Because your body cannot store protein, which is constantly wearing out, you need a regular and reasonably good supply of this vital macronutrient. When you perform a physical activity, especially a strenuous one, many cells in your body are broken down. New ones are built up only with protein.

For those who eat animal flesh, the best kind of protein is that which is low in fat, such as white chicken and turkey breasts as well as fish. For people who consume red meat like beef, they should likewise focus on the lean variety. If, however, you detect a lot of fat in any meat you buy, trim off as much of it as possible. Saturated fat is dangerous to your health. Vegetarians, on the other hand, may get their protein from three excellent sources: (1)tofu (2)soy imitation meat products such as soy hot dogs and hamburgers (3)protein isolate powders. The protein in these three are highly concentrated as compared to the traditional peas, beans, and lentils that also have a great amount of carbohydrate, and part of the protein from them is not digested (and therefore not absorbed) because of their high fiber content. So take these factors into account when eating the latter. Also, if you consume cheese and milk, beware of the saturated fat. It's better to use the low-fat kind.

Regarding **fat**, the body requires a reasonable amount of it to keep you warm, store energy for future use, release energy as needed, regulate body temperature, provide healthy skin and hair, protect vital organs such as kidney and heart from blows and trauma, and provide a protective covering to the nervous system. However, you must choose the correct type of fat to put into your system. It's definitely not saturated fat but monounsaturated fat. The highest concentration of this kind of fat is found in olive oil, olives, almonds, cashews, pistachios, macadamia nuts, and avocado.

Exercising

Exercise helps keep the body fit, healthy, and strong. There are basically two types of exercises: aerobic and anaerobic. Aerobic simply means exercising with air (oxygen) and anaerobic signifies exercising without air (oxygen). More specifically, in aerobic exercise, the rate of oxygen transfer to the cells is great and sustained, as the person does moderate-intensity exercise over a fixed period of time. This makes for aerobic metabolism. Whereas anaerobic exercise does not focus on an ongoing flow of oxygen but requires a quick, explosive burst of energy. Building endurance and burning fat are the primary benefits of **exercising aerobically**. Some examples of this kind of exercise are walking, jogging, swimming, cycling, and skipping rope. If you were to walk for half-an-hour every day, six days a week or jog for three days a week at one hour a day, your body will be getting the ideal amount of aerobic exercise. If you find it difficult to spare the time, seize every opportunity you can to walk. For instance, climb the stairs instead of taking the elevator, or park your car some distance from the office and walk.

Doing some stretching exercises before an aerobic workout is an excellent habit to cultivate. You may stretch your neck, shoulders, arms, chest, back, abdomen, buttocks, and legs. Stretching will enable your body to become more flexible, avoid muscle damage, and help you develop greater strength. Wild animals, imprisoned in cages, maintain powerful bodies and sound physical health by stretching themselves.

The main advantages of **anaerobic** or resistance exercise are building muscles and strength. Weight lifting, push-ups, and chin-ups are forms of anaerobic training. When the exercise becomes strenuous and you push yourself to the limit, then you get the fullest benefit from resistence training. These benefits include the release of human growth hormone to rebuild the microscopic tears in your muscle tissue, the development of lean muscle mass, and greater strength.

It's a good idea to cultivate a sport, such as tennis, football, basketball, etc. But in these forms of activities, the swift upshoot of energy makes them largely anaerobic instead of aerobic exercises. Muscle cells switch to anaerobic metabolism. This means the energy is conserved in the absence of oxygen where fat is no longer used to generate more energy.

Wisdom dictates that you do a combination of aerobic and anaerobic exercises. The end result will be a healthy, fit, and powerful body.

Resting And Being Positive

Resting is just as important as eating proper foods and exercising. Get enough sleep. Enough varies with each individual. Some may need eight hours; others, seven or six. Find out your cycle of sleeping. Don't work long hours without resting and don't skip meals. While on vacation, forget about work. Just enjoy yourself in a natural and spontaneous way that's often not permitted in the work environment. To help you do so, learn to experience inaction in action. That is, operate from a center of stillness from within you. And you'd find, to your great delight and joy, that little or no tiredness will overcome you even when your activities are physically demanding.

Very important for physical health also is developing and maintaining **a positive mental attitude** as well as attaining mastery over your thoughts and emotions, especially your negative ones. This is because your thoughts and emotions have a direct impact on your body.

B. EMOTIONAL/AESTHETIC DIMENSION

The human body is a battlefield wherein is waged a war between positive and negative emotions. In our age, the latter seem to be winning. Everywhere we turn, we see people governed by hate, anger, greed, etc. You often wonder where have the positive emotions of love, kindness, and joy fled.

Negative emotions can harm us psychologically, socially, physically and spiritually. Psychologically, these emotions result in various types of mental disorders. Tension, anxiety, and general disorientation have a field day. In our social relations, discord results when we express hate and anger towards others. Also, our physical health can be badly impaired. For example, excessive worry can result in peptic ulcers and skin diseases. Finally, in spiritual terms, negative emotions turn into a screen of darkness within us. This darkness covers the divine light inside us.

On the other hand, positive emotions help us generate true, all round health and happiness. The person who displays love, self-confidence, generosity, etc. draws to himself the positive forces of the universe. Thus, it's desirable to practice positive emotions and rid yourselves of negative ones. You may use some or all of the methods and techniques discussed in chapter 4 to enable you to overcome negative emotions and develop positive ones. Learn also to conform to the great **law of harmony or balance**. That is, operate from that deep silence within you and sometimes, as the occasion demands, rise above all emotions. To help you do so, practice the Equilibrium Method as specified in chapter 4. Self-mastery brings with it joy and power. However, self-mastery is largely determined by emotional mastery.

In addition, your life becomes richer if you have developed your aesthetic sense. This sense has to do with the perception and enjoyment of beauty in its many forms. For example, you may enjoy the beauty of nature, art in its many varieties, and great music.

Regarding the emotional/aesthetic side of life, don't forget that thoughts and emotions or feelings are closely related. Your thoughts will sooner or later transform themselves into their corresponding emotions. Thus, imbue your personality with positive thoughts and you'd become a positive force field - a human dynamo generating a positive and constructive influence in your environment. On the other hand, negative thoughts create a negative force field around you that may also cause you to become a human dynamo but rearing for discord, enmity, and even destruction.

C. MENTAL DIMENSION

You use this aspect of your personality much of your waking life. You employ it to think and plan. How you speak and act also determine your level of mental development.

You may set goals in this area after assessing your strengths and weaknesses. Are you a curious person? That is, do you possess a curiosity to find out and learn more and more? All great people – scientists, inventors, writers, etc. – have developed this trait to a remarkable extent. Only the individual who's constantly learning and improving will become outstanding. For life is changing all the time.

Do you keep abreast of current events, new developments, or research in your field? If you don't, vital parts of your knowledge will become out-dated with devastating effect to your professional reputation.

Are you mentally stimulated enough? Do you feel deficient in areas that are important to your success? Many people perceive the gaps but do nothing. You must develop a thirst for knowledge if you wish to excel in this information age.

Do you listen carefully to others?. By doing so, you'd increase your knowledge. This is because everyone has something important to offer. Each person sees the world with unique eyes. Life has taught him/her at least one thing well.

Here are some suggestions that will help you in your mental development. One, pick at least one area of study that fascinates you.

Then, learn all you can about it. To know one thing better than anyone else will greatly help you to earn the respect of others in that particular field. Also, the knowledge will help you generate enthusiasm and assist you in developing an exciting personality.

Two, think about how the different forces in society are influencing people for the better or worse. The whole world, due to mass communication through various technological breakthroughs, has become an electronic community. The latest entertainment video, for example, reaches the remotest areas of the world through satellite communication. Also, significant happenings in America affect the entire globe. For example, shudders on Wall Street, New York, have a spiraling effect all over the world. As the Dow Jones plunges, all the other major stock exchanges follow suit in a short while. Note, therefore, that only through understanding can our lives be meaningfully and intelligently directed.

Three, take steps to upgrade your education and expand your mind. You may do so by reading books, journals, and magazines; looking at educational videos; using CD's; listening to specialized audio cassettes; and tapping into the vast storehouse of knowledge through the internet. Also, take courses relevant to your needs and listen to experts in selected areas. Sometimes, a new interest or hobby brings hours of satisfaction and even financial rewards.

Four, evolve a philosophy based on your experiences and aspirations. Think about yourself in relation to those around you and the world. Develop a global outlook that transcends color, creed, and race. Formulate a few basic principles that are meaningful to you and around which you may revolve your life. Bring the separate strands of your existence together. If you revolve around your life certain basic values, your whole existence will become internally consistent. Then, you life will be well-integrated and thus conform to the great **universal law of harmony or balance**.

D. SOCIAL/FAMILY DIMENSION

Social Dimension

Are you so pre-occupied with your work that you forget about social life? If this applies to you, your existence is one-sided. You'd sooner or later feel a gap or vacuum within you. For the saying that people are social animals has much validity to it. Of course, in some jobs your social need is fulfilled to a certain extent. In other work environments you feel alienated. To help you satisfy your basic social need for companionship or rootedness, while pursuing an interest, join a network or create one. There are thousands of networks all over the world in a wide variety of different areas (i.e.) crime prevention, sports, health, ecology, helping the poor, consumer protection, human rights, spiritual development, etc.

While socializing, it's wise to maintain a balanced, yet pleasant posture – neither too friendly nor hostile. Your personality must be flexible to cope with changing situations. Observe others and respond appropriately. Be friendly when it's suitable; be firm when the occasion requires it.

You should adopt a proactive approach by consistently working towards improving your relations with people. Here are several ways of doing so: have an open mind; learn to see things from the standpoint of others; take a keen interest in people; smile genuinely; develop the habit of remembering the names of others; pay attention when someone is speaking with you and respect their opinion; take it easy on criticisms; give people credit for helpful actions and constructive ideas; and bring out the best in those who have the good fortune to come your way.

Family Dimension

If your family life is crumbling, you can never be happy. But if a feeling of love and togetherness is felt, you're most likely managing this area of life very well. Also, if you have a very good family life, your social need for companionship will be satisfied. However, having a social life outside the family will certainly broaden your horizon.

To know if you love your family and are taking good care of them, answer the following question and those that follow. Do you find out the needs of each and help to satisfy them? Helping to satisfy a person's needs is a concrete expression of love.

Do you spend enough time with members of your family or are you always too busy doing other things? Make sure when you're at home, you're present in body and consciousness. That is, don't occupy your attention with work when you're with your family. Ensure the time spent is quality time. If you reflect long and hard enough you can think of many ways to make life for your family exciting, challenging, and meaningful. Help all of them develop their potential to the fullest, feel good about themselves, strive towards excellence in their chosen fields, master inter-personal relationships, and be exposed to new, enriching experiences.

Here is a friendly word of advice. Do not be unfaithful to your partner. Unfaithfulness fosters guilt and interferes with your development. Also, you may end up with prolonged psychological problems for yourself, and social ones in relation to your children.

Do you have a nagging spouse. Remember that at the root of nagging is one or more unsatisfied need(s). You must help satisfy your partner's needs while working towards a harmonious relationship. This approach will assist in creating a pleasant atmosphere which will benefit all.

Have you helped your children work out their future vocation in line with their interests and abilities? Remember that one of the best gifts to your child is ensuring that she/he learns a skill, becomes a professional, or be set up in business. You'd be doubly blessed for seeing to it that your daughter or son becomes financially self-supporting.

E. FINANCIAL DIMENSION

Ideally, you should choose an area you love from which to earn a living. Why? If you really love something, you may be motivated to master it better than anyone else. When this happens, your financial problem is permanently solved. However, if you're not able to develop this high level of expertise, you can still become a reasonably good success in your particular field. This you may do by steady, persistent, enthusiastic work. Learn to enjoy every step towards your goal. Don't give up if difficulties arise, and remember that a regular, systematic approach is the best means of mastering anything. Formulate your short, mid, and long term financial goals and set plans in motion to accomplish them.

Are you satisfied with your income? If you're not, don't moan; do something about it. For instance, you may upgrade your knowledge and skills or change jobs. In addition, you may consider doing something on the side. I once met an electrical engineer several years ago who was struggling to support his wife and six children on his salary. He ventured into part time sales – selling a computerized service after work. With a radiant glow on his face, he told me that he made $30,000.00 in one year from this extra job. Besides, there are people who started businesses in their basements and ended up as roaring successes.

Do you manage your money properly? You should try to save a part of your income every month, if you're on a salary. However, if you're working on commission or are self-employed, save a part of your money as you get it, no matter how small. Once your savings build up and you have some kind of capital base, you may consider investing in a diversified portfolio. You have a wide choice: individual stocks and bonds; mutual (investment) funds; registered retirement savings plan (RRSP); cash instruments (savings, guaranteed investment certificates, money market funds); real estate (especially a comfortable home); gold; etc. Remember that your investments should be based on a careful assessment of your financial goal(s) (i.e. whether you're investing for income or not), your age, the size of your family and the age of each member, the amount of risk you can afford to take, the economic conditions prevailing at the time, and an intelligent long-term projection for the future.

Don't forget that one of the big secrets to becoming financially wealthy is through the magic of compound interest: allowing interest to pile upon interest. For example, if someone invests $10,000.00 in a mutual fund which yields an average annual return of 12 percent, his investment will double every 6 years. Let's say at age 23 he invests this sum of money. By the time he retires (at age 65) his $10,000.00 initial investment will be worth $1,280,000.00.

Regarding mutual funds (investment funds), stick with the ones that have a long, solid track record. Through investment funds most people get the opportunity to invest in stocks. However, this form of investment is for the long term. One of the best ways to invest in mutual funds is putting in a regular sum of money every month – as little as $100.00. In this way, you'd benefit from dollar-cost-averaging. It means you'd use the peaks and valleys of the stock market to your advantage and in the end emerge a winner. How does dollar-cost-averaging work? When the market is low, your money for that month will buy more share units; when prices rise, your monthly contribution will buy less shares but your overall portfolio will be worth more. Wise investing in mutual funds for 30-40 years will allow you to have a comfortable retirement. Your funds will weather the ravages of all kinds of market downturns and will eventually realize substantial gains. However, it is very dangerous to speculate in mutual funds – going into them to make a quick buck and get out. The probability of losing money in the short term is extremely high.

If you really want to make money, there is always a way to do so. Some people, with little or no capital, have accumulated a fortune through the use of initiative and creativity. I read a true story several years ago involving two engineers who became unemployed. They were forced to use their creative resources to ward off starvation after trying unsuccessfully to find jobs. They discussed their plan with the manager of a bank who decided to provide them with some capital. Their idea was to create an artificial beach. They dug up a large area, arranged it in varying depths and concreted it. Then they filled it with water and installed machineries that they themselves had invented.

Their mechanical devices were made to spin the water into waves. They charged each person a fee to bathe. Soon, thousands of people were coming. Their customers needed food, temporary housing accommodation, and gas. Thus, they extended their businesses to restaurants, beach houses, and gas stations. The result was that these destitute engineers were transformed into multi-millionaires.

Also, look at money in its correct perspective – as something through which your needs are satisfied, not as an end in itself. Never allow it to control you. Your aim is to achieve freedom, not to put yourself in bondage. Remember that money, properly used, can bring yourself and others great blessings.

Finally, use the making of money as a means to develop yourself to a higher level. You can do this by putting in an extra effort to help those who are involved with your work to be happier and more successful. Focus on excellence of service, while working in a flow of joy, with love for those with and for whom you work and let the radiant beauty of your Spirit light up the environment.

F. RECREATIONAL DIMENSION

Making a living is tough for most people. Many are working in areas through necessity, not choice. They don't enjoy what they do and perceive their work as meaningless. The recreational dimension is especially important to these people. Here they may exercise their freedom by choosing something they enjoy, while (if they so desire) developing their skills and abilities.

For hobbies or special interests there are a multitude of choices, such as: sports; games; social work; entertainment: music, singing, dancing, and acting; education: learning a foreign language, reading, writing, teaching, etc.; adventure: flying a plane, scuba diving, sky diving, mountain climbing, traveling to various countries; opening a business; spiritual development; crafts, such as knitting, pottery; and household skills: cooking and gardening, etc.

It is possible that your enthusiasm for a hobby builds up so powerfully that you end up spending lots of time and effort pursuing it. As a result, you may find yourself becoming a great expert in the area. Then, lo and behold! you now have a new and fascinating career. This is exactly what happened to Charles Darwin, the biologist who developed the world shattering theory of evolution. Darwin studied divinity and was going to be a priest, but his passion was biology which he pursued relentlessly. In our own time many people who took a great likeness to computers at the early stages turned their hobby into a fortune. The most noteworthy example is Bill Gates who, according to the July 5, 1999 issue of Forbes magazine, accumulated a personal fortune worth 90 billion US dollars through his software company, Microsoft.

G. MORAL/SPIRITUAL DIMENSION

Everyone needs peace or inner satisfaction. Do you find time for prayer and meditation? Prayer works fastest when you use some of the principles that govern the subconscious - desire mixed with repetition, faith, and visualization. Your subconscious more often gives you the answer than any external agency, though the intervention of outside forces is possible.

Do you try to express love instead of hate? Love is the emotional manifestation of Truth. Love is the thread that emotionally connects all humanity. Do you look for the best in people and bring it out instead of indulging in destructive criticisms? Bringing out the richest potential in others is one of the greatest work you can ever hope to do. Do you sometimes help others for no gain? Remember that unselfish work is one of the great secrets of spiritual development and other benefits. This is directly in keeping with the **law of harmony or balance**. Whatever you send out comes back to you.

Are you an honest person? Honesty is a tremendous virtue. However, be discreet. See that you don't stab anyone with it.

Do you consider all people your brothers and sisters? Remember that a spark of the same Universal Truth or Force resides in everyone. In this way, the human race is inextricably linked. Develop, then, a universalistic viewpoint wherein you transcend all barriers of class, creed, or race and penetrate to the heart of existence.

ASSIGNMENT: Here is an assignment for the reader that will prove very useful. Using the outline given at the beginning of this chapter, set goals for yourself in the seven dimensions or areas of life. Then write down your goals in order of priority. As you accomplish a goal, set up and start working on another. Learn to see success as an ongoing process rather than as something fixed. Review your goals in all areas once a month. As you begin to achieve goals in the seven dimensions, your life will automatically become more balanced, integrated, meaningful, energized, and happier.

CHAPTER 8

Laws or Principles of Success and Human Development

The laws or principles of success and human development distil the essence of this book. Thus, some repetition of previous material is unavoidable. Keep in mind that to succeed in anything, you must look for the law or principle that governs that thing and use it. Also to understand any area of life, seek out the underlying laws or principles. This approach will help you better come to terms with situations, people, and nature. It will open up the well-guarded door of wisdom to you.

1. REPETITIVE PRACTICE OR LAW OF EFFORT

Only by repeatedly practicing something can you ever hope to master it. Nature has locked into this **law of effort** one of the great secrets of success. If you wish to achieve excellence in any area, you must toil in the vineyard of life; there is no other way. Something for nothing does not exist in the reality of human existence.

Why does regular practice work? It does, because as you practice something over and over again, nature causes a deep and thick electrical tract for that thing to develop in your brain. This tract, when it reaches a certain vibrational intensity or critical mass, taps directly into an Energy Field. It's this same Field that provides the power for the martial arts expert to break bricks with his bare hands, and athletes to smash records. It also supplies the wisdom, through the same law of effort, for scientists to make breakthroughs or outstanding artists to produce creative, path-breaking works.

This Force Field is also filtered through the human agency, when called upon, in the form of intense emotions. For example, just keep practicing love and joy everyday and you'd see what will start happening to you. To help you practice love, look for something you like in everyone you meet and make them feel great about themselves in your presence. With respect to joy, sometimes let go your heavy cares and become like a little child. Look at everything with refreshed vision. Be spontaneous: laugh, express yourself naturally in speech and behavior, and notice how simple and exhilarating everything becomes.

Nature has also decreed that to be effortlessly competent in anything you must work at it diligently. Notice how many painstaking hours of hard work the musician, athlete, scholar, etc. must put in to attain that easy and natural flow of perfection or near perfection.

2. REPETITIVE SUGGESTION

Whenever a suggestion (whether it comes from yourself or someone else) is presented to you long enough, it will eventually influence your thoughts and behavior. Thus, one of the secrets of success is to practice using verbal self-suggestion. That is, repeat to yourself over and over again whatever you wish to accomplish. By this means, the suggestion will move down into your subconscious mind, which will show you a way to achieve your goal.

By seizing the initiative and programming your mind with goals in the seven dimensions of existence, your life will take on greater direction, focus, and meaning. In addition, you'd become success-oriented to a greater extent. One of the worst things you can do is leave your mind idle. If you do this, negative thoughts will keep filtering through it and cause you to develop failure patterns and a wide variety of problems.

3. NATURAL JUSTICE OR KARMA

The law of natural justice or karma states that as you sow, so shall you reap. Good thoughts and deeds eventually bring you positive results. Harmful thoughts and deeds come back to the sender with negative results. Therefore, keep a watchful eye over your thinking and action. For, your negative thoughts will pass through your central nervous system and do you injury, and action geared to hurt others contains the seeds of retribution. If the other person does not respond in kind, he will not be affected. For many years this author has been observing the fascinating law of justice in motion. This is what he discovered on many occasions: a person tries to harm someone through words or deeds and some time later (a few hours, days, weeks, months) another individual does him the same thing he did to his victim.

4. ASSOCIATION

The mind functions through the law of association. Similar thoughts link up one by one until a whole chain of thoughts develops. A positive chain of thoughts influences your personality positively; a negative one affects your personality negatively. Remember that just one negative thought can trigger off such a long series of disturbing thoughts from your **negative memory bank** that you may end up very depressed. On the other hand, one positive thought can release such a chain of desirable thoughts from your **positive memory bank** that you may find yourself in a winning state of mind. Your success, to a large extent, depends upon such a positive state.

In addition, if you want to remember something, just associate it with something you already know. If you wish to retain it for a long time, make the association so ridiculous that the uniqueness of it may stand out in your brain for a lifetime. For example, if you must remember a pen and a bicycle, just visualize the pen riding the bicycle.

5. REINFORCEMENT

This law states that behavior continues and is strengthened when suitably rewarded. At the beginning, if you want someone to establish a particular form of behavior, reward that behavior continuously – that is, each time the individual behaves in the desired way, reinforce or reward it. However, once the behavior has taken root, reinforce it intermittently – that is, sometimes reward the behavior and at other times, don't. In this way, the person doesn't know when the reward is coming, so he continues the behavior pattern. This is one reason why some people get hooked on gambling - experience has taught them that, even though they're losing, they can start to win anytime.

Rewards can take two forms: tangible and intangible. Examples of tangible or extrinsic rewards are: money, medals, trophies, certificates of recognition, etc. Intangible or intrinsic rewards may be given in several ways. For example, a company may cause someone to feel a sense of belonging by making him/her feel a part of a select group (i.e.) employee of the month. People may also be praised for constructive ideas or work well done. This form of reward will boost their self-esteem. In addition, the reinforcement may take the shape of giving them meaningful and challenging work so that their potential may be more fully realized.

6. IMAGINATION OR CREATIVITY

Imagination is the creative faculty. Whatever you wish to create or bring into physical manifestation must first be clearly visualized, often repeatedly. For example, if you want to have a house built, you must first visualize its form and then have a plan of it drawn before building it. It was Edison's vision to light up the whole world that brought, to a certain extent, into reality the incandescent light. It was also an act of vision by someone that preceded the landing of man on the moon. Imagination is the source from which springs creative expression in all aspects of existence.

7. CONCENTRATION

Powerful concentration on any area of life, over a prolonged period of time, brings success or mastery in that area. In fact, concentration is one of the master keys for succeeding in anything you choose. All great people, without exception, have been able to develop deep concentration. It is by means of this intense focus that outstanding works are produced in all fields, and seemingly insurmountable problems solved.

8. SUBCONSCIOUS OR FAITH

Faith or belief in the power of the subconscious to bring about any result is the master principle or law governing success. This law states that whatever your mind completely believes will come to pass. The subconscious will accept it, speed up its rate of vibration so that it draws power from Supreme Intelligence or the Absolute. Then a point of no return will be reached in the sense that the particular thing will be brought into fruition. To build faith, which is difficult to come by, use verbal self-suggestion and visualization, as was explained earlier. In connection with faith, note well the following point: a basic or central issue in life is whether we believe in ourselves or not, whether we live a life of faith or fear.

9. BALANCE OR HARMONY

Nature does not allow extremes to continue for long. Anything flung out of balance eventually moves back to a state of harmony. For example, many university students, confined to studies for several years, suddenly develop an insatiable urge to travel all over the world. Bear in mind also that if you're using the intellect too much and neglecting the emotional side, nature will force a crisis upon you. This crisis will result in the expression of much emotion. It may be triggered by almost anything (i.e.) experiencing a death in the family, separating from your spouse, etc. As human beings, we must form a balance between the heart and head to experience our fullest humanity. Excellence in any field also results from tapping this law, whether it be in painting, the martial arts, or human relations.

10. UNITY/ONENESS

All life strives toward unity and may be seen in terms of interrelationships and interdependencies. For example, the lover yearns to unite with his/her beloved. All rivers move irresistibly towards the ocean and become one with it because they're part of the ocean. And most important of all, humankind is one through the same Force that binds all people. Thus, the emotional manifestation of this Force, the transcendental power of love, can greatly help in bringing alienated humanity together again.

Unity or oneness is also an important principle of success. For example, teamwork is an essential foundation for business success. All must pull together in the same direction. Remember also that it's very unlikely for one person to become wealthy working alone. The individual needs the knowledge, skills, abilities, and experiences of others with whom a success-oriented group can be established. The combined effort of this group, if intelligently and harmoniously directed, will produce the desired results.

11. SUITABILITY

To succeed in anything, you must say and/or do what is suitable or appropriate at the time. To operate in this manner, you ought to understand the situation and speak or act in accord with it. Listening, looking, and thinking before speaking and acting will certainly help in pointing to you what is suitable.

12. SILENCE OR STILLNESS

From a profound center of stillness within, the greatest insights emerge, and most powerful action erupts. Excellence in expression also occurs from tapping this silent, eternal spring of energy. While acting from this inner silence, you become an instrument for the manifestation of that Supreme Power that underlies all existence. Like a whirlpool that appears still but generates tremendous force, your inner self is capable of inducing volcanic activity amidst a calm exterior. Therefore the paradox of action in inaction, and inaction in action becomes understandable.

13. ECONOMY OR PARSIMONY

Economy in speech or action, when geared toward a specific objective, hits the target directly. Long-windedness and wasted movements make for inefficiency and ineffectiveness. To help you conform to this law, ask yourself two questions: (a) What is the objective of my communication (when oral or written communication is the medium of expression)? (b) What can I do to cut down wasted or unnecessary movements – in other words, how can I achieve my goal in the shortest and most effective way? (when action is the issue). The general rule for adhering to this law is to keep it short and simple. Note that some of the simplest theories have led to staggering breakthroughs. For example, Einstein's equation $E = MC^2$ (Energy = Mass times the speed of light squared) contributed to the dawning of the atomic age.

14. POLARITY

The wise person learns to bring polarities in a working relationship or delicate balance within his/her life: polarities, such as reason and emotion; activity and passivity; joy and sorrow etc. This law urges people to experience both poles in life to feel a sense of completion. How do you apply it? An example is, if you're too joyful about something, calm down and remember the times you were in a state of sorrow. Whenever the use of cold reason is making others uncomfortable, stop and express love by showing genuine concern for the needs and viewpoints of others.

15. FEEDBACK

Appropriate feedback, given in a spirit of genuine helpfulness, makes for self-understanding and contributes to personal growth. Accurate feedback, especially from someone you trust, can cause you to do self-assessment which may lead to personality improvement and greater effectiveness in your daily life. Thus, put aside egotism and listen to others on how you're affecting them and how you're performing. Keep an open, flexible mind and you'd be greatly helped in having an enriched, learning experience. Life is like a school in which we're learning lessons all the time. When you apply the idea of continuous learning and improvement to your life, you will work wonders for your personal development and overall success.

16. GROWTH THROUGH SUFFERING

Much growth comes about through struggle and pain. After the suffering, if one searches carefully enough, one gets an opportunity to rise to a higher level of development. However, the insight must not only be intellectually grasped but applied in day-to-day life. The biographies of great men and women indicate that before they rose to the top, they were severely tested by life. In fact, many of them reached such a low point that they thought they would have been completely destroyed. To apply this law, ask yourself: "What can I learn from this seemingly unfortunate experience and how can I apply the lesson to improve my life?" For example, an overworked business executive so neglected his wife that she ended up divorcing him. The pain and suffering of this experience resulted in his making a resounding success of his second marriage. A callous businessman lost his millions during a recession. The result was that he identified more closely with suffering humanity and developed a more caring and compassionate attitude towards others.

THE HEART OR KERNEL OF THE BOOK

1. **The organizing principle of life is Truth.** This Truth or Force is what connects all life together. It's the basic underlying principle of existence. This Reality is like the sun and we're like rays that sparkle from this sun.

2. **The goal of life is to realize Truth or the Absolute and act in accord with It** in such a way so as to succeed in all areas of our choice. Associated to this two-fold goal are two basic states: the absolute and relative. The absolute state comes about through profound silence, whereby we become aware of our connection with Truth. It's a direct experience of the Source without acting. Whereas in the relative condition,

we're deep in action. This Force empowers us to focus actively on our goals.

3. **The main universal law pervading all life is Oneness.** All matter consists of the same basic scientific element (the atom with its electrons, protons, neutrons, and other smaller particles). In addition, Truth or one Energy Source pervades all existence. In silence we may become aware of our connection with It; in love we become one with It and perceive all humanity as our brothers and sisters.

4. **The proposed theme at all levels of society is cooperation or unity.** Through sharing and support we may be able to pull this planet together again. Then peace and harmony will have a better chance. This does not mean that competition ought to be eliminated. There should always be room for healthy and fair competition.

5. **The ideal person is the unified person:** one who has integrated and balanced within himself/herself the three aspects of personality and seven dimensions of existence. This individual also moves through life in a concentrated flow while experiencing existence as a unity.

CHAPTER 9

Integrating/Balancing/Unifying the Three Aspects of Personality and Seven Dimensions of Existence in Day-To-Day Life

1. Have the three-aspect model of personality in your mind and periodically evaluate yourself against it to ensure you are applying the three elements: knowledge/wisdom, feeling/emotion, action/power. Do the evaluation at least once every twenty four hours, preferably at night.

2. How can you integrate the three aspects of personality in practical life? Act from a deep inner silence (let no thoughts intervene). This combines action with wisdom and results in powerful concentration: you're connected to the Force when you're silent and from this connection all wisdom flows. You may bring together knowledge (intellectual) and love when you figure out the need of someone and listen with interest and caring to the expression of that need. Action and love join forces when you do something for a person out of the purity of your heart, with no thought of personal gain. The intellect (knowledge) is combined with personal power (action) when feedback is given to an individual whose speech and/or behavior is affecting you negatively. When you let him know how the provocative remark or action is affecting you, the chances of his putting an end to it become very high. However,

the feedback should be given from a calm rather than an angry state of mind.

3. How do you integrate wisdom/knowledge, feeling/emotion, and action/power in meditation? First, meditate on silence for connection to the Source (realized knowledge or wisdom). Follow this up by meditating on love. Just feel unconditional love for yourself, everyone on the planet, and the Supreme. You're simply loving the one Essence that pervades everything. Then meditate on personal power. Visualize pure white light entering the top of your head from above and moving through your whole body. See every cell lighted up and feel a powerful surge of energy vibrating continuously through you. Afterwards, let go and be silent, allowing the three aspects of your nature to merge into one at a higher level.

4. Check at least once a month to see to what extent you are achieving your goals in the seven dimensions of existence: physical, mental, emotional/aesthetic, social/family, financial, recreational, and moral/spiritual.

5. In family life, help your spouse and children balance the three aspects of their personalities and achieve goals in the seven dimensions of existence.

6. In inter-personal or group relations, use the three elements of personality. For example, exercise reason (intellectual knowledge) to figure out what is appropriate or suitable to say or do at the time. Draw upon intuitive knowledge, especially

during an impasse, by being silent or still and seeking guidance from the Source. Again, bring into play the emotional/feeling aspect by expressing love in its purest form – helping others to satisfy their needs (i.e. for survival, belonging, justice, respect, esteem, and self-fulfillment or actualization). Finally, use will or power by exercising firmness or control when the necessity arises (i.e.) by cutting off irrelevancies or senseless bickering and moving the group directly towards agreed-upon objectives.

7. How do unified people view and deal with the material and spiritual sides of existence? To them, both are interrelated and real in their own way. They feel at home in both worlds by harmonizing the relative (practical) and absolute in thought and action.

CONCLUDING REMARKS

In the annals of recorded history, 20th century civilization had no comparison in material wealth, science, and technology. Yet the world hovered and still hovers (at the beginning of the 21st century) on the brink of disaster. The United Nations, created after World War II, to prevent armed conflicts, has witnessed dozens of major wars. The Middle East, Africa, and certain parts of South America and Eastern Europe have turned into boiling cauldrons. The danger of a third world war is now much less with the crumbling of one of the super powers. But the testing of nuclear weapons by India and Pakistan in May 1998 and their intense conflict over Kashmir serve as a serious warning signal for the future.

Yet another war has begun: a titanic struggle for economic supremacy among the U.S.A., Japan and Germany. This fierce economic battle will continue to be waged from three powerful bases: the North American Free Trade Agreement (NAFTA) led by the United states; the Association of South-East Asian Nations (ASEAN) headed by Japan; and the European Union (E.U.) with Germany as the lead country. These nations will also continue to operate through the capitalist or free enterprise system which was also the dominant economic system of the 20th century. The big advantage of capitalism is that it's based on the freedom of all individuals within society to pursue their own economic destiny. The great disadvantage is that it makes for the concentration of wealth in a few highly developed countries. Not only that, only a small percentage of people in these industrially-advanced countries become wealthy through the dynamics of this market economy. For example, according to a report by the UN Human Development Programme released on July 12, 1999, the combined wealth of the world's richest three families surpasses the assets of the 600 million people in the least developed countries. Also, the assets (over one trillion U.S. dollars) of the world's 200 wealthiest people account for more than the combined income of 41 per cent of the earth's population.

Related to this theme of poverty and wealth is the whole question of globalization, which involves the collapsing of space, time and borders through information technology and the internationalization of capital. Globalization has the potential of greatly lessening poverty or further widening the rich-poor gap. Through exchange of technology, knowledge, goods and services, all participating nations could be better off. However, many emerging countries have found themselves seriously handicapped or facing economic catastrophe because of not having the proper regulatory controls (or not enforcing the ones in place), infrastructure, and management to run a market economy effectively. Also, some degree of global controls are necessary in a world where, through a few clicks of a computer keys, the wealth of an entire nation could be wiped out in a matter of seconds. In addition, widespread political corruption in many developing countries is deterring much-needed investment from several of the developed nations. Voters therefore need to choose their leaders more wisely.

While the rich countries are busy pursuing their own self-interest, the poor ones are struggling for financial survival. About 80 percent of the world's population, mostly concentrated in the latter countries, live in poverty. From a humanitarian standpoint, from the need to create a safer world, and from self-interest (creating larger markets consisting of people who could afford to buy their goods and services), the wealthy nations should help the disadvantaged ones. They could assist in the following ways: through multinational corporations (that do most of the business-applied research and create most of the technological patents) allowing these countries to use their new technology without paying an exorbitant price for its use; by offering the people fairer wages in their branch plants (where they are not already doing so) instead of exploiting them; by working with them to develop effective safeguards and infrastructures necessary for the proper functioning of a market economy; by providing private- sector investments; and giving more government aid for health, education and economic development.

Within the context of our social, political, and economic global environment, what is really happening at the people level? There are hatreds, fears, frustrations, and bitter conflicts at all levels: international, national, in cities, organizations, families, etc. Racial antagonisms and religious bigotry run riot on the planet. And, with the upsurge in international terrorism, no one is safe, not even innocent civilians in aircrafts and around embassies.

The question arises, "What can we do in the present situation?" To know what to do, it is necessary to understand a great underlying message of history and nature. The lesson from history can be detected from analyzing humankind's three civilizations: agricultural, industrial and the present post-industrial or electronic one. The trend has been an increasing move towards globalization until today the world is like a global community. Through the telephone, television, telegraph, computer, internet, and fax machines, communication becomes instant from one point of the planet to any other. What, then, is the lesson or message? Is not our electronic or information civilization indicating to everyone to adopt a global or universalistic perspective? And does not such a perspective signify the breaking down of sectarian barriers of race, religion, creed, and ideology? Is not the force behind history telling us it is time to open up by accepting people as brothers and sisters despite their differences?

And, what is the underlying message of nature? It is closely related to the message of history. Bear in mind that man (woman) has, for thousands of years, not changed from the standpoint of his (her) physical evolution or development. May not nature be telling us that the next great pathway for evolution should be in the development or unfoldment of consciousness? However, this time it may have to be rapid evolution or transformation to catch up with our breathtaking revolution in science and technology.

Thus, it appears that the great message or lesson of history and nature is for people to focus powerfully on human development - the unfoldment of consciousness and the establishing of effective human relations. Only if people raise their levels of consciousness can they begin to develop a global perspective by transcending the barriers of religion, race, and ideology that so fiercely separate them.

The basic problem, however, is inherent in the fact that material development generally, and science and technology specifically, have by leaps and bounds outstripped human development. This gap has resulted in a lot of social disorganization and psychological problems. If it's not adequately bridged, catastrophe awaits us. But what have humans been doing, over the past several thousand years, in this critical area of human development. The answer is, very little in comparison to material development. In this area, they have generally operated in a hit and miss fashion. The approach has been mostly unorganized and unsystematic.

This author is therefore proposing a more serious focus on human development throughout the planet. It should be geared towards speeding up humankind's inner evolution. It ought to take into account both the scientific model of the West and the intuitive, meditation model of the East. Using only one approach has resulted in people from both civilizations developing in a one-sided manner. For example, the highly developed swami or yogi may have conquered the inner kingdom by unfolding his consciousness to a remarkably advanced level. However, he may end up broke and have to rely on others for a living. This happens if he neglects the material side of life. On the other hand, the successful westerner, who's concentrating almost exclusively on financial success, may end up acquiring an enormous fortune. However, he may find himself experiencing inner poverty, besieged by a host of psychological problems. He conquers the external kingdom at the expense of the inner one. Both personal development and achievement are necessary to survive with dignity on this planet. We need a more balanced, integrated, or unified approach. All aspects of individual and social life must be explored and fully developed. Everything that affects human development should be examined. **What is here advocated is a revolution in human development, to parallel and interact with our scientific and technological revolution**, that could produce a vastly improved 21st century civilization.

However, right now, we need a new world view in tune with our recent, post-industrial civilization. The world is not an impersonal machine, as proposed by Bacon, Descartes, and Newton. This view prevailed in the previous industrial civilization and has since been contributing to disastrous consequences in the lives of humanity. Many people in large cities have, since the industrial revolution, been moving about in a machine-like or robot-like condition. That is, they have been experiencing an inability to express emotions with a feeling of alienation or social isolation. Thus, a more appropriate perspective is to view the world as a living, open system that is not separate and independent from people. All things must be seen in terms of interrelationships and interdependencies, not mechanistically but organically.

Another aspect of this new world view is to see man/woman as a vibrant being with varied needs and motivations. However, he/she should be viewed as a unified or whole person with the search for meaning or Truth as central to him/her. This means that a certain conception of John Locke and Adam Smith is inadequate for our times. They saw man as a propertied or self-seeking being. This perspective dominated industrial civilization. In addition, Darwin's view of the fiercely competitive nature of all living beings, including people, needs some re-examination. A greater focus on cooperation and teamwork can work wonders for our planet. Notice the dramatic rise of Japan as a post-industrial nation in a very short time partly due to effective teamwork at all levels of their society. This is not to say we ought to eliminate all competition, but only to suggest that we should form a healthy balance between cooperation and competition.

A third facet of this new world view is to see planet earth as a living single cell or world community in which the following are made to prevail. One, the ecology is treated with dignity and respect, with a focus on the greening of the environment rather than its pollution. Two, all systems and technologies are used as supports for the welfare of people. Three, everyone and every nation are interdependent and should therefore focus on mutual development (a shared approach). Four, there should be a constant balance of polarities: independence and interdependence, cooperation and competition, reason and emotions, etc.

However, remember that, in your pursuit of human development, you should also relax and enjoy yourself. Take delight in whatever you do. Go outside and have a leisurely stroll, as the refreshing breeze of spring caresses your skin; spontaneously react to a glorious summer's day: the sparkling sunlight, the enchanting blue sky, the stirring melody of birds, the wonder of flowers, and the lush vegetation; drink in the beauty of the multi-colored autumn leaves; and feast your eyes on the pure, white snow as winter casts its magic spell all around. Or, if you prefer, sit quietly in silence, or play a sport or game just for the fun of it, without caring whether you win or lose. You may also listen to music that inspires and relaxes you. In addition, have a night out with family or friends just enjoying one another's company without talking about work or anything negative. Also make humor a part of your life. Learn to laugh at yourself, so you may not get so uptight at criticisms. Look for the funny side of existence in your day-to-day life. Watch comedy shows through videos or movies and you'd soon loosen those heavy cares you've been carryng around. Read books on humor and, at every opportunity, listen to the master humorists. Share jokes with those with whom you're interacting, but make sure the timing is opportune and the joke is appropriate. After all, we were put on earth to live out so many years. We may as well balance life's sorrows with life's enjoyment. For, in the end, all we're left with from our stay on this planet are our memories or experiences.

In parting, may I wish you great success in your efforts at personal development and achievement. As you progress, remember to help others. Each of you may light even a small fire. When these little fires are combined, such a conflagration will burst forth that the entire course of civilization will shift in a more positive direction. Then a golden age will dawn unprecedented in the annals of recorded history.

INDEX

Absolute, 23, 108
Acton oriented, 66
Action Research Model, 14-15
Aesthetic, 87
Africa, 113
Age, Golden, 120
Association of South-East Nations(ASEAN), 114
Attitude, positive mental, 86

Bacon, 118
Balance, 104
Beauty, 10

Capitalism, 114
Carbohydrate(s), 82-83
Cheerfulness, 11
Civilizations
    agricultural, 116
    industrial, 116
    electronic, 116
Columbus, Christopher, 20
Communication, effective, 15-18
Concentration, 24-25, 69-70
Consciousness, 23

Cooperation, 11, 109
Creativity, 103

Darwin, Charles, 96, 119
Depressive-oriented, 8
Descartes, 118
Development-oriented, 8

Eastern Europe, 113
Edison, 103
Egotism, 42-43
Einstein, Albert, 20, 106
Emotions
    origin of, 39-42
Emotions and qualities, conquering negative ones and building up positive ones, 49-55
    Dynamic Positive Method, 50-52
        Mirror Technique, 50
        Positive Imagination Technique, 50
        Imagination Action Technique, 51
        Action Technique, 51-52
    Dynamic Reversal Method, 52-55
        Instant Reversal Technique, 52-53
        Imagination Reversal Technique, 53

Rational Technique, 53-54
Affirmation Technique, 54
Equilibrium Method, 54-55
　Positive emotions and qualities for development
　　prudence, 46
　　patience, 46
　　persistence, 46
　　assertiveness, 47
　　love, 47-48
　　compassion, 48
　　decision-making, 48-49
　　enthusiasm, 49
　The 20 main negative emotions and qualities, 42
　　egotism, 43
　　anger, 43
　　hatred, 43
　　revenge, 43
　　malice, 43
　　mercilessness, 43
　　injustice, 43
　　impatience, 43
　　intolerance, 43
　　fear, 43
　　worry, 43
　　imprudence, 43
　　vanity, 43
　　dishonesty, 43
　　hypocrisy, 43
　　envy, 43
　　greed, 43
　　lust, 44
　　cowardice, 44
　　undependability, 44

Energy, 23
　Central Energy Source, 23
　Cosmic Energy Field, 23
　Field, 99
European Union (E.U.), 114
Evolution, rapid, 117
Existence, The 7 dimensions of, 79-88
　emotional/aesthetic, 86-88
　financial, 92-95
　mental, 88-90
　moral/spiritual, 96-97
　physical, 81-86
　recreational, 95-96
　social/family, 90-92
Excellence, 10
Exercises
　concentration, 25-28
　meditation, 30-36
　relaxation, 28-30
Exercising, 84-85
　aerobic, 84-85
　anaerobic, 85

Faith, 73-74
Family, 91-92
Fat, 84
Feedback, 20-21, 66-67, 107
Force, 23
Force Field, 100

Gates, Bill, 96
Germany, 114
Globalization, 114-115, 116
Goals, 63-64, 79-81

God, 23

Harmony, 104, 109
Human development, and science and technology,
    The gap between, 1, 117

Imagination, 72-73, 75, 76, 103
India, 113

Japan, 68, 114
Japanese, 68
Joy, 10
Justice, 9-10

Kashmir, 113

Leader, 69
Life, Philosophy of, 5-6
Locke, John, 119

Market-oriented, 68
Meals, well-balanced, 82-84
Meditation, 23-24
    meditation exercises, 30-36
Middle East, 113
Mind, 23-24

Newton, 118
North American Free Trade Agreement (NAFTA), 114
Nuclear weapons, 113

Other-centered, 67-69

Pakistan, 113
People, dealing with difficult, 16
Person, unified, 3, 109, 113
Personality, The 3 aspects of, 3, 111-112
    action/power, 3, 4, 111
    feeling/emotion, 3, 4, 111
    knowledge/wisdom, 3, 4, 111
Pleasantness, 11
Perspective, universalistic/global, 117
Polarities, balancing, 11-12
Poverty, 115
Practice, regular, 70-71
Proactive, 64-65
Production/oriented, 68
Protein, 83-84
Psychotherapy, 68

Relaxation, 71-72
Resting, 86

Self, 4, 23, 25
Self-suggestion, verbal, 72, 74-76, 101-102
Selfishness, 42
Sherman, Mendel, 39
Situational approach, The, 18-19
Smith, Adam, 119
Source, 23
South America, 113
Spiritual, 96-97
Subconscious, Laws of the, 71-74
Suggestion, auto, 72, 74-76, 101-102
Supreme, 23
Success and human development,
    Laws/principles of,

law of effort, 99-100
repetitive suggestion, 100-101
natural justice/karma, 101
association, 101-102
reinforcement, 102-103
imagination/creativity, 103
concentration, 103
subconscious/faith, 104
balance/harmony, 104
unity/oneness, 105
suitability, 105
silence or stillness, 106
economy or parsimony, 106
polarity, 107
feedback, 107
growth through suffering, 107-108

Transformation, 117
Truth, 4, 9, 23, 108

United Nations, 113
Unity, 11, 12
U.S.A., 114

Visualization, 74-77, 103

Watson, John B., 39
Wealth, concentration of, 114
World view, new, 118-119